WHY WOMEN NEED TO NEGOTIATE

Negotiating is a part of life. Whether you like it or not, negotiating is often the only way to get what you want. Tough negotiators don't give people power over them. Women must learn to be tough.

SUCCESSFUL NEGOTIATING SKILLS FOR WOMEN

IS PACKED WITH REAL-LIFE SITUATIONS AND SPECIFIC DOWN-TO-EARTH TIPS.

"With the step-by-step organization of this clear and efficient book, negotiation can be part of the working repertoire of any woman. Clear and concise, this book is highly recommended."
THE WEST COAST REVIEW OF BOOKS

"You don't have to settle for less. SUCCESSFUL NEGOTIATING SKILLS FOR WOMEN is an important handbook for getting what you want."
WORKING WOMAN

SUCCESSFUL NEGOTIATING SKILLS FOR WOMEN

JOHN ILICH and
BARBARA SCHINDLER JONES

PLAYBOY PAPERBACKS

Nothing in life is to be feared.
It is only to be understood.

Marie Curie

Preface

The idea for this book was suggested by Richard J. Staron, Addison-Wesley Senior Editor. He had worked with both of us on other books and recommended a collaboration. In bringing us together, Dick saw the value of our combined backgrounds: John as a lawyer and experienced, highly successful negotiator; Barbara as a communication consultant interested in women's issues. We readily agreed that there was a need for a book to help women be better negotiators.

Why should *you* care about negotiating? Some women look puzzled or indifferent when the subject of negotiation is raised because they see little relation to them and their lives. Both men and women are apt to recognize negotiation only on the highest, most visible levels, such as international disputes, labor-management contracts, or corporation sales and mergers. Yet negotiation is a part of our daily existence and transpires in small and sometimes unexpected ways. Your car might not start on the day after the warranty expires. You might decide to have your house painted, but the estimate is two hundred dollars over your budget. You might need a loan but can't afford an interest rate that is too high. Your teenager might want an increased allowance when he or she has not done the chores you assigned. You might arrive at the airport in plenty of time but discover you have been bumped off the flight.

These examples and many more could be classified under "Daily Frustrations" or "Life's Like That." But then what? Unless you constantly give in to other people's wishes and thus give them power over you, or unless you use bully tactics to get what you want, *your only recourse is to negotiate*.

More business and career opportunities exist for women than ever before, and these are bound to increase and widen in scope. In addition, women who choose careers as housewives and mothers are assuming greater responsibility for family decisions, decisions that often involve large sums of money and far-reaching consequences.

With their emergence into new fields and acceptance of new challenges, women need to acquire knowledge that will enable them to make better decisions and compete more effectively. And because many of the problems or situations that women will encounter will be unique to them, it follows that a negotiation book written especially for women will greatly assist them in the successful conduct of their business and personal lives.

Why negotiation? Because negotiation is, in essence, the art of dealing with people, and for a woman to enhance her chances of success in any endeavor, she must become proficient in this art. As she weaves her way through her personal life and up the business, professional, political, or governmental ladder, the key to success will to a great extent depend on her ability to deal with people.

This book covers in detail those situations and problems that a woman can be expected to encounter and explains how to successfully apply to them the art of negotiation. To fully illustrate the suggested strategy or process, the text contains many examples, most of which have been drawn from personal experience. The ideas in this book have been thoroughly tested and successfully practiced. They are offered to today's woman (and perhaps the man looking over her shoulder) to assist her in successfully attaining her goals.

Grand Rapids, Michigan   J.I.
Boulder, Colorado   B.S.J.
June 1980

Contents

CONTENTS

CHAPTER 1

Why a Special Book on Negotiating for Women?

The answer, in addition to what already has been related in the Preface, further lies in all the complexities of attitudes and values surrounding the changing role of women. In the past, woman was expected to be the helper, the subordinate, the power *behind* the throne. With all their new options for changed thinking and behavior, many women find themselves exhilarated and challenged—but unprepared.

PAST CONDITIONING HAS CREATED PROBLEMS

Over the years, society (meaning both women and men) has dictated what the role of women is and how they are supposed to behave. The fact that different societies have promoted different male and female roles substantiates the conclusion that the roles are based on social rather than biological factors.

In the United States, the emphasis has been on being "lady-like" and passive, to be chosen rather than to choose, to follow rather than to lead. But times are changing quickly. Women are competing more and are learning it is possible to be both feminine and successful. Yet some women are still receiving mixed messages. Be ambitious and assertive but don't be *too* ambitious or assertive.

Women have been conditioned, too, not to speak up and to avoid conflict. As one woman put it, "I'll back down in a minute if I think someone is going to bristle at me or have their feelings hurt. I was raised to nurture and be nice to everyone, not cause pain."

Part of the conditioning process has involved unquestioning acceptance of idealistic principles. Myth #1: The world is a fair place. Myth #2: Good things will happen if you just do your job and work hard. Some women are hurt and shocked to learn that, unfortunately, fairness does not abound, especially in the business world, and that all too often virtue not only goes unrewarded but isn't even recognized.

An example of specific conditioning is "math anxiety." This term is more than a catch phrase; it is a condition that has prevented people from advancing in many professions. Sheila Tobias, head of a consulting firm that treats the panic, muddled thinking, and inability to concentrate characteristic of math anxiety, notes that even the simplest entrance exams test logic and numbers. People afraid to tackle even basic math problems cut themselves off from drawing up budgets, analyzing finances, and using computers.

Legions of young women contracted math anxiety when they were counseled not to take courses in higher mathematics or the hard sciences on the grounds that such courses were too difficult. Even more damaging was the message that women would have no use for such information. Recently, for example, an advisor (female) was overheard telling a female college student, "You won't need calculus to figure out how many square yards of carpet to order or how to change the quantities in a recipe. Calculus is for boys."

Another restrictive attitude women have acquired is that negotiating, particularly when money is involved, is a male domain. Women have willingly (and gratefully) allowed their fathers, brothers, bosses, and husbands to make life and financial decisions for them rather than learn how themselves. Now, however, since women can get credit in their own names, and hold property in their own rights, more and more women are beginning to make their own decisions, necessitating that they do their own negotiating.

LOW EXPECTATIONS BRING LOW RESULTS

For centuries women have been conditioned to help others aim high but to have rather low aims themselves. If you don't expect much, you get used to accepting less, and anything above your expectations seems like a windfall rather than a right.

Expectations are judgments related to the role

we assume and are based largely on our past experiences. Since expectations are in our heads and not in reality, they can be changed.

As we will see in later chapters, expectations have a way of coming true. What we aim for is often what we get. Yet for a variety of reasons, women have been reluctant to set clear-cut goals and objectives for themselves or to consciously make deliberate choices among their increasing options. Your expectations of success cannot be high if you aren't sure what you want or what you're willing to do to get it.

LACK OF INFORMATION HAMPERS

Too frequently, women lack information and don't know where or how to get it. Going into negotiations without an arsenal of facts and figures is starting out unarmed and vulnerable. Some people are reluctant to ask for information, fearing they will appear inept or stupid.

MANY WOMEN LACK SUPPORT SYSTEMS

On the winds of change has come the realization that women need to establish "Old Girls' Networks," to operate in the same way that the proverbial Old Boys' Network has. Women have not had the same access to guidance, encouragement, or information as men have.

Yale Professor Rosabeth Moss Kanter commented on this problem in a recent interview:

I often hear male executives complain that a woman seems to "top" her aspirations at a lower level than a man does. I always question whether the context for ambition is the same for men and women. Often a man will find greater acceptance and more security as he goes upward in the organization, whereas a woman moving up will find that she will get less and less support over time.[1]

A very important form of support can come from mentors—older, more experienced men or women who can guide and advise and even pave the way. Successful men often credit a mentor for giving them a leg up the ladder.

Women, on the other hand, find they usually have to go it alone. Few have had true mentors to help.

Of the women interviewed about their attitudes and experience with negotiation, however, those who reported they *enjoyed* negotiating and felt they were good at it, all said they had early positive role models or highly supportive relatives or friends. Most of their mentors were male, usually fathers or husbands and occasionally colleagues. One woman explained how she enlisted the aid of two male colleagues to give her support and honest feedback. The men have helped her see many aspects of management she hadn't understood. They even coached her on how to prepare her case when she negotiated a raise.

---

1. "Corporate Success: You Don't Have to Play by *Their* Rules: A Conversation with Rosabeth Moss Kanter," *Ms.*, 8 (1979): 63–64, 107–109.

WOMEN OFTEN COMMUNICATE FROM WEAKNESS

Some women may not negotiate well because they are timid (we have suggestions to counteract and overcome timidity in Chapter 5); but even women who are not timid, who feel strong and secure, may speak in a way that communicates a lack of power and credibility.

Research on the differences between the way men and women talk reveals that women are more apt to (1) use flowery, empty adjectives like "divine" or "lovely"; and qualifiers like "sort of" and "kind of"; and (2) end sentences with questions like "don't you think?" or end a sentence with a questioning tone, such as, "I think what you're looking for is over there?" Men interrupt far more than women do and more frequently give shorter answers or no response at all. In these ways, men control conversations and hold on to power.[2]

In Barbara's consulting work she sometimes coaches professional women on how to improve their voice tone and pitch and other nonverbal aspects of their speech. No matter how intelligent the person, a light voice with a tentative tone communicates uncertainty and lack of confidence. Thin, weak vocal quality is not apt to be heard or taken seriously.

"No one accepts my ideas in a meeting—it's as if I'm invisible," managerial women may complain. But when they hear and see themselves on

2. See Mary Brown Parlee, "Conversational Politics," *Psychology Today*, 12 (1979): 48–55.

videotape, even they must admit their way of communicating lacks credibility and conviction.

IGNORANCE HAS BEEN AN EXCUSE (BUT NO MORE)

Some women have not been successful negotiators because they didn't know they were supposed to negotiate. As an example, Barbara's first professional position was as an assistant advertising manager in a large corporation. She was so pleased to get the job and especially to break out of the secretarial pool (in another company) that she accepted the salary offered and felt truly blessed. It wasn't until two years later when she decided to quit and the boss began offering her more money to stay, that she realized how naive she had been. Only then did she discover that the two male assistant advertising managers were making much more money than she and that she probably could have had more too had she known she *was expected to ask for it*. You can't be expected to play a game by the rules if you don't know those rules—or that you're even in a game!

So these are additional important reasons why a special book for women has been written: to help you redo your attitudes and approach; to help you raise your expectations; to help you establish a support system; to help you improve your communication and, above all, provide knowledge and know-how that will enable you to compete effectively in whatever you choose to undertake in our highly competitive society.

CHAPTER 2

Why Women Need to Negotiate

Some people call negotiating bargaining, some call it haggling. Others explain negotiating as the process of arriving at cooperative agreements. Some practitioners of the art distinguish between bargaining and negotiating by limiting bargaining to interaction over a sale or purchase and broadening negotiating to involve complex social units and multiple issues.

Negotiation takes place whenever there is a conferring or interaction between individuals, whenever somebody is trying to persuade someone else, whenever ideas are exchanged in an effort to influence thought or behavior. Usually, however, negotiation occurs over something specific, such as a product for sale or a service to be rendered, and that is the context for this book. We are not talking about the art of persuasion or successful communication between people *in general;* but in the specific act of negotiating an agreement, a sale, a contract, or something similar.

Negotiating is an ongoing, dynamic, everchanging procedure. Yet, there are often unwritten rules about the steps to be taken, when and by whom, depending upon the objective and the context of the negotiating. When is it appropriate, for example, to walk away? When are you expected to make a counteroffer? These factors are well known to experienced negotiators but beginners may be in the dark. Sometimes the negotiating steps, such as in labor-management contracts, are ritualistic and are taken in well-planned, well-rehearsed sequence and timing. Women who have not been schooled in the process of negotiating or have had little opportunity to experience what goes on from the inside, are inevitably vulnerable to manipulation and failure. This book is intended to change that.

Here are some sample illustrations.

1. *Buying a product in a store*

When about to buy a product, the potential buyer can begin the process of negotiating by looking at the price tag and then saying to the seller, "The price is too high!" Five simple words that can make a big difference, words that tell the seller, in effect, "I'm interested but let's talk about a lower price." The next steps involve the necessary give-and-take between the asking and selling price until both parties agree.

2. *Buying a product at a foreign bazaar or flea market*

   a. "How much is it?" you ask, then show dismay at the obviously inflated price. Your simple facial expression will be "telling" the seller that the price is too high.
   b. Chances are good that the seller will then ask how much you are willing to pay.
   c. You then make a lower counteroffer.
   d. The seller may then register dismay as part of the role playing, but will probably make a counteroffer lower than the original price but higher than yours.
   e. You then adjust your price upward as the seller moves down until you reach agreement.

3. *Problem-solving negotiating*

   a. Start with a statement of what needs to be negotiated.
   b. Point out the consequences of not negotiating.
   c. Determine the best possible and also the least acceptable solution or strategy.
   d. Develop a solution or strategy within these limits.
   e. Sell the solution or strategy.

Before we close the subject of the *process* of negotiating, we want to emphasize the importance of the *social interaction* and the cultural aspects involved. Negotiators need a sense of humor along with quick wits and verbal skill. They need to remember their manners and whenever possible, help their opponent to save face.

One of the women interviewed reported that she didn't like taking the time to negotiate because she always wanted to get right down to the bottom line. But she said she behaves differently when traveling in Mexico because she feels it insults the merchant not to engage in the social interaction of bargaining. Her experience has been that Mexican merchants would rather take less money than skip the ritual exchange. The social exchange is important *in itself*.

One final but important thought. The term *opponent* is used to designate the person or group you are attempting to negotiate with. This person may even be your best friend but is nevertheless the competitor.

WHY DO WOMEN NEED TO NEGOTIATE?

Some of the women interviewed said they found negotiating "scary," "embarrassing," or "demeaning." "I had to learn to be tough," said one. "I had to learn to be unafraid of walking into a situation without knowing what's behind the door. I've learned to push myself, ask questions and not take no for an answer."

Women are rapidly learning the ropes and changing their attitudes about the positive attributes of power and negotiating. These are no longer dirty words in female vocabularies.

We all (women and men) need to negotiate because it is a part of human interaction and a part of our way of life, whether we like it or not. Negotiating is a way (often the *only* way) to get what we want. It is a way to make progress and improve our position. It is a way to deal with people and of increasing our skills in human understanding and interaction.

Aspects That Apply to Virtually All Negotiating

Certain aspects of negotiating apply in virtually all situations. They are:

1. Using leverage
2. Effective communication—both verbal and nonverbal
3. Setting
4. Timing

USING LEVERAGE

Leverage can be illustrated by visualizing a person attempting to move a large rock by placing a pole under the rock with a smaller rock set at the base of the pole and then pushing down on the pole to lift and move the rock. The longer and stronger the pole, the greater the leverage and the easier it is to move the large rock.

The same is true in negotiation. The greater the leverage you use, the easier it is to accomplish your negotiating objectives.

For example, consider what a successful photographer did to collect overdue bills from customers. He would go through his files and find the worst picture or proof of the customers he had and include it with the bill. Also with the bill was a note advising the customer that if the photographer received permission to display this picture of the customer in the photographer's window, the photographer would consider the bill to be paid in full. Usually, the photographer received payment of the bill shortly thereafter.

What the photographer did, of course, was to employ leverage, namely, the customer's fear that if they didn't quickly pay their overdue bill, they would be unfavorably displayed in the window for everyone to see.

The degree or amount of leverage to employ will vary according to what you determine is necessary in each negotiating situation as will be illustrated in subsequent chapters. What we are stressing here is the need to use leverage in negotiation to help you attain your negotiating objectives. Successful negotiators are always on the lookout for ways to strengthen their leverage and to use it when the timing is most favorable.

EFFECTIVE COMMUNICATION—BOTH VERBAL AND NONVERBAL

Communication is, of course, the essence of negotiation, just as it is a central part of everything we do. Human interaction succeeds or fails as a direct function of our ability to communicate.

But there is purposeful communication and there is also inadvertent communication. For example, you may present your qualifications to a prospective employer in a firm, clear, well-modulated voice but the unconscious clasping and unclasping of your hands betrays nervousness that could be interpreted as lack of confidence.

Communication as an ongoing, dynamic process cannot be stopped. We can't *not* communicate. There is no such thing as noncommunication because all behavior has some kind of message value. Whether or not we are able to ascribe the right meaning in all situations depends upon our skill and experience.

Listening

Of all the communication skills, listening is the one we use the most and also the one that is the most difficult. Hearing with our ears, being aware of sound, is fairly easy. But true listening involves the mind. Listening effectively means screening out distractions and concentrating both on what is said and what is not said.

The mind must be involved in *evaluating* the information to which you are listening, *predicting* what will come next, *reviewing* the main points covered, and *remembering* key ideas for later use and response. All this while you are still listening! You lose if you tune out the speaker in order to think. As the listener, you must adjust to the speaker's rate, not your own.

Most of us are not taught to listen in the way we were taught to read. Instead, we taught ourselves by imitating the way our parents and teachers appeared to listen and also by trial and error. Along the way most of us picked up some bad habits. One bad habit is using our time to think of what we want to say next instead of concentrating on what the person is saying. Another is assuming we know what the other person is going to say, so we don't really listen. Still another is hearing what we want to hear instead of what is actually being said. Finally, a fourth bad habit is faking listening attention (with a nod here and an "Uh huh" there) while letting our minds drift away.

A Word About Silence

Some people are uncomfortable with silence and feel they have to say something to fill it. But successful negotiators realize the value of silence and do not feel they must be constantly talking. You can gain not only useful information but also control by encouraging your opponent to talk freely while you listen carefully.

For example, when John recently negotiated the purchase of investment property for a client, the seller's representative provided the basic information on the property such as the offering price, the property dimensions, and the present zoning. But John also hoped to learn how badly the seller wanted to sell, so he asked some general questions about the seller. The seller's representative was very talkative and volunteered many details about the seller's present status and future plans. By listening carefully, John obtained important information that was ultimately helpful in the negotiation.

Using Questions in Negotiation

Another communication skill is knowing how and when to ask questions. There are numerous advantages to posing questions during the course of any negotiation:

Questions can be excellent probing tools to discover additional facts and other information that may only be known to an opponent or otherwise extremely difficult for the negotiator to discover.

General questions are useful for probing and are best during the early stages of negotiation. As matters unfold, however, it is usually better to refrain from asking them in order not to run the danger of reopening already agreed upon items, or to unfavorably reflect upon the negotiator's thoroughness of preparation or grasp of the subject matter. In addition, a wise opponent may be able to detect when the negotiator is attempting to strengthen her own knowledge by general questions, and his or her response may therefore not be too enlightening.

Specific questions are much safer to venture out with, since they call for fairly confirmed answers. They're useful in any phase of the negotiation, but more so in the latter stages when the negotiator is more apt to know precisely what she is after when asking. . . . There should always be an objective at the end of every question, whether it be general or specific. Asking merely to be asking or to satisfy curiosity is never to be recommended.

Whether a question is general or specific, it should be carefully phrased and descriptive in order to have the greatest impact. Descriptive questions will provide the opponent with more of a mental picture of the answer to be elicited. Contrast "Where is the property located?" with "Is the property located near transportation, adequate labor supplies and ample utilities?" The latter question is obviously more illustrative of the negotiator's objectives and thus more likely to draw a productive response. In addition, being a more specific question, it doesn't permit the opponent to ride all over the range with his or her response and perhaps be evasive or even seize the offensive.[1]

Being a skilled interviewer is a decided asset to negotiators. But little is accomplished if the question-asker *fails to listen to the answer*. Be careful not to mentally leap ahead to the next question or worse to interrupt the person before the answer has been completed unless, of course, your interruption is a matter of negotiating strategy.

---

1. John Ilich, *The Art and Skill of Successful Negotiation* (Englewood Cliffs, N.J.: Prentice-Hall, 1973), pp. 141–145.

Feedback

A corollary to both listening and asking questions is the ability to give and get feedback. We give feedback when we respond in some way to what the other person is saying. Getting feedback means we are alert to all the messages coming our way. When we are unsure of the meaning, we don't guess but seek clarification.

During negotiation you must not be shy about asking what the other person means. A question like "Do I understand you to mean such and such?" tells the other person that not only are you a good listener but you want to avoid the trap of assuming understanding rather than checking it out.

Communication is aimed at shared meanings. Because *people* mean (not words) and because we all have layers of connotations, experiences, and unique pictures in our heads, the successful communicator pays more attention to what people *mean* than to what they say.

Words do not have meanings, nor do words contain meanings as a glass might contain water. The container concept is one of the most damaging misconceptions about words. Maybe you have said, or heard someone say, "I'll look that word up in the dictionary and see what it means." But dictionaries give us definitions, not meanings. Definitions tell us what most people have agreed the symbol represents. Meaning, on the other hand, is highly individual and personal.[2]

---

2. James Gambrell Robbins and Barbara Schlinder Jones, *Effective Communication for Today's Manager* (New York: Lebhar-Friedman Books, 1974), p. 36.

Nonverbal Communication

Of great importance in a negotiating context, as we have already seen, is the whole realm of non-verbal communication, which includes all the messages that go along with or instead of words.

The thrust of a hitchhiker's thumb, the feel of a clammy handshake, a sarcastic tone of voice, the lift of an eyebrow, and rapid footsteps on the stairs are all messages.

These and many other nonverbal messages are so pervasive and subtle that we may not even be aware that we are responding to them. A friend smiles at our joke and we continue with new enthusiasm. Our listener frowns and we begin to adjust what we are saying, trying to make the frown go away.

Research shows that 65 percent of the meaning of any two-person conversation comes from the nonverbal rather than the spoken word. The most obvious of the many possible cues come from posture and facial expressions and tone of voice.

We can learn to watch for and do a better job of interpreting the myriad signs and signals involved in communication. But we must be cautious about attaching meaning, particularly intended meaning, to nonverbal clues. If we work or live with someone and can observe them in different contexts, we can begin to understand and read the nonverbal messages accurately. For example, certain puffiness around a spouse's eyes is a sign of tiredness; the boss's tapping of a pencil indicates that the boss is impatient and wants the meeting concluded. But generalizing from the signals to other people's nonverbal communication, such as deciding that every time someone taps a pencil he or she is impatient, is risky and may lead us to false conclusions.

1. Appearance

Your opponent will form judgments about your capability and credibility, largely from your appearance. Your clothes should reflect professionalism as well as your own taste and style. For business purposes, women are usually advised to wear a suit or a blazer with a skirt. No flashy patterns or loud designs; these may distract rather than convince. Neatness counts; attention to grooming pays off.

One executive woman in a large corporation says wearing suits sets her apart from the other women in the office. Since she is small, she wears styles and colors that make her look bigger.

Dark glasses should be avoided unless they are necessary for medical reasons (and if that is the case, say so) because dark glasses give an image of distrust and secrecy.

Don't forget that the appearance of the materials you use is also important. A briefcase says you mean business and if the papers inside are neatly arranged, you have communicated you are well organized. One of the women interviewed explained that her technique was to use an expensive looking notebook in which she had written reminders about all the points she wanted to make. "In this way," she explained, "they *feel* my preparedness, and I have set the stage for the negotiating."

Also, you should evaluate the appearance of

your opponents' materials for their communication value. A lawyer related that she took the risk of advising her client, the seller of a house, to get up and leave the negotiating session because of the sloppy and incomplete set of papers presented by the buyer and the buyer's representative. The tactic worked and the sale was completed at the next meeting, with the seller maintaining the upper hand.

2. Voice quality and control

We have already stressed the importance of developing vocal strength and projection so you do not sound unsure or lacking in credibility. Consciously work for a lower pitch because high-pitched, squeaky voices reflect nervousness and lack of power. Vocal variety is another plus because monotones tend to put people to sleep.

3. Eye contact

Although eye contact behavior and its interpretation vary in different cultures, Americans usually equate a direct eye contact with honesty, directness, and confidence. Since eye contact is viewed as the most powerful of nonverbal messages, people who avoid direct eye contact communicate uncertainty and deference.

Looking your opponent directly in the eye communicates several things. It says you are unafraid; it says you care if the opponent is listening to you; and it also provides you with essential feedback about how well you are getting through, including whether you need to modify your communication efforts for greater clarity or persuasiveness.

4. *Use of time*

How do you feel when someone keeps you waiting? Annoyed? Put down? Or grateful for a few minutes to relax and catch your breath? Punctuality or tardiness are messages negotiators need to use to their advantage. But be sure you communicate the message you intend.

If you have studied your opponent and know how that person feels about punctuality, you can choose your best approach. For business appointments, people can be five or ten minutes late without excuse, but if they are much later than that, they must be wary of what their lateness is communicating. The best policy is to be on time.

5. *Use of space*

We all have private bubbles of space that we do not like intruded upon except by invitation. Age, sex, and ethnic background influence the size and importance of that personal space. Be careful about the other person's turf, however. You can annoy someone by sitting too close (or too far) or even by moving an ash tray to one side. Be alert to clues about other people's comfort or discomfort and make them work for you rather than against you.

SETTING

Where the negotiation takes place is an important factor. If at all possible, choose the place in which you are most comfortable, your "home field," which might be your office or your home or even your car. The home field advantage is well known in sports. Being on familiar ground also is best in negotiation because you are more at ease and because you will be able to concentrate more effectively and not need to spend energy adjusting to new and different surroundings.

The next best place would be a neutral setting such as a restaurant or any other suitable place. Obviously, you want to prevent your opponents from enjoying the advantage of negotiating on their home fields. If, however, you are not in a position to choose the place, you need to be flexible enough to negotiate wherever you have to, even if that means on your opponent's home field.

TIMING

You should attempt to control the time of the meeting and select a time when you are the most effective mentally. If, for example, you do not really begin to function until after ten o'clock in the morning it would be to your advantage not to begin any negotiation earlier.

With experience you can sense when the time is right and also when it is wrong. Don't try to negotiate a raise, for example, if the boss is obviously in a grumpy mood or just got word of a drop in sales. Some people, unfortunately, get themselves so "psyched up" to go after something, they become deaf and blind to the messages that shout, "Not now!"

There may be situations in which you have no choice about the time to negotiate. It's now or never. You should therefore seize the opportunities when they are presented even though the timing may not be perfectly suited to you.

CHAPTER 4

General Negotiating Advice

To add to the underlying aspects covered in the previous chapter, here are some general dos and don'ts. All are important both from the standpoint of attaining consistent negotiating success and from the resulting personal growth that sustains such success.

SET GOALS AND TARGETS

Without goals, negotiators set sail for an unknown port. If you don't know where you're going, how do you know when you get there? The target should not be vague or ambiguous such as "I'm hoping for a good deal," or "I want to wind up with more money." Goals should be specific and clear. "I want that loan for no more than 7 percent interest," or "I want a salary increase of at least 8 percent."

You cannot negotiate effectively unless you have carefully thought through what it is you want and *are willing to ask for it*. As we say in Chapter 1, many women have been conditioned to passively accept rather than actively seek change.

Many women have not asked for what they want or need, frequently on the false assumption that the other person is a mind reader who *ought to know* what they want or need. These same women also may have bought the myth that if they continue to do their best, someday they will be rewarded, which is often not the case unless they are willing to speak up for what they want.

Most women I talk to admit reluctantly that they "never asked for a raise in their lives." No wonder they're not getting paid. . . . Everybody who is worth anything is *expected* to play the game.[1]

You need to recognize that your negotiating opponents are neither mind readers nor philanthropic. It is therefore important that you clearly identify what you want, learn to think in terms of specific goals and targets, and then go after them.

SET YOUR OWN NEGOTIATING STANDARDS

You should strive to set your own negotiating standards rather than try to copy other people's. You may possess tremendous negotiating potential

---

1. Betty Lehan Harragan, *Games Mother Never Taught You: Corporate Gamesmanship for Women* (New York: Warner Books, 1977), p. 237.

that far exceeds that of the person you are trying to copy. So if you base your standards upon that other person, you may be setting them too low.

Another temptation is to try to outdo others, especially men, perhaps with an I'll-show-him attitude. Avoid this temptation.

You should objectively examine your own abilities and potential and set your negotiating standards based upon the results of your analysis. This method will enable you to better recognize and reach your negotiating potential.

DO NOT BE AWED BY EXPERTS

President Truman defined an expert as "a fella who was afraid to learn anything new because then he wouldn't be an *expert* anymore."[2]

You may encounter all types of experts during negotiation, including real estate, financial, legal and appraisal professionals. When you do, the most important point to remember is not to be awed by them. Don't set them on a pedestal and accept everything they say. On the contrary, treat them as objectively as you would anyone else. And above all, do not hesitate to question them or their written reports. Bear in mind that what they are advocating is normally their own opinion, which even among experts can vary widely. Real estate appraisals are a good example. In most instances, if you had twenty appraisers independently appraise a piece of real estate, each would probably arrive at a different value.

2. Merle Miller, *Plain Speaking* (New York: Berkeley Publishing, 1973), p. 216.

BE PREPARED AND NEGOTIATE IN SPECIFICS—NOT GENERALITIES

Lack of information, as we discussed in Chapter 1, makes for a weak negotiating position. Analyze the situation, the stakes, and the opponent to spot any gaps in your knowledge. When you apply for a new job, for example, you won't be able to successfully negotiate a starting salary if you don't know what the going rate for that position is. The more you know ahead of time, the stronger your negotiating stance.

For consumer purchases shop around so you are able to quote specific prices and compare model information. Resist grabbing the first item or option encountered.

Too often in negotiation, generalities are accepted and used as the basis for action. For example, John recently negotiated the purchase of a large parcel of investment property for a client. The real estate broker spoke highly of the potential of the property in general terms and even related that there was an apartment development nearby that would increase its value. The broker then sent a written note that said the broker had *"reason* to believe" that the seller *"may* have turned down" a very high offer at one time. (Emphasis added.) Notice how general the statement is, certainly too general to influence any decision on whether to purchase the property or how much to offer. Upon actually visiting the property, John learned that a great portion was really not usable because it was divided by natural ravines. This specific knowledge was indispensable in ascertaining the real value of the property and what negotiating position to adopt.

You will be bombarded with generalities in many of your negotiations. You simply cannot accept statements like "reason to believe" or "may have turned down" as a basis for making your negotiating decisions. Consider generalities only as a starting place from which to gain more specific information.

LEARN TO KNOW YOUR OPPONENTS

An important target for your advance research is obtaining knowledge of your opponents. What are they like? What are their attitudes, values, and experience?

Knowledge of your opponent can be enhanced considerably by combining as much as you know about your opponent with your overall knowledge of people. For this reason you should try to meet as many different types of people as you are able to within your personal activities. If you broaden your experience with people and combine that experience with reading, particularly in the areas of psychology and history, you will eventually possess an excellent understanding of people that will pay off.

Travel is another excellent way to learn about all kinds of people. The more you travel, the more you will find that people possess the same basic emotions but differ in degree in the way they display those emotions. One person, for example, may cry at a funeral. Another person may not. Yet both may have the same relationship to the deceased and the same feeling of bereavement. This degree of difference is what you should concentrate on detecting so that you will be able to understand your opponent better.

Although there are variations, the following are capsule sketches of the three basic types of opponents you will encounter.

The strong type

These people are daring and unafraid. They like to control things and frequently interrupt, often anticipating and answering questions before they are fully asked. They may forgive but seldom forget. Such people make decisions quickly and confidently, even if they later turn out to be in error. This is one of the best ways to spot them. There are very few gray areas in their way of thinking: everything is generally either black or white. They seldom err because they prepare well. They are able to analyze well, but their haste in making decisions often offsets this. Their appearance is generally very neat and precise; this is another good way to spot them. They take pride in how they look and carry themselves as if they want others to know it. They anger quickly and may even become angry when a position that they feel is reasonable is not accepted. On other occasions, they tend to feel sorry for themselves for the same reason. This is why it is very important to explain in detail the reason or reasons any of their positions are not acceptable, and to always treat the arguments seriously even though they may appear unrealistic to you. This type of individual is very easy to lead, particularly if your positions appear either black or white. They are very responsive to reasonable suggestions or to positions that have been amply substantiated by facts, laws or other means.

The vacillating type

These people are very similar to the strong type, but differ in the following important respects. They are generally not as dynamic and prefer to think things over. They seldom interrupt. They anger quickly but forget just as quickly. They like to consult outsiders or experts and like to refer to them during discussion. This makes it harder to close. It's important, therefore, for your positions to be well substantiated in order to get them to make decisions. Although these people are just as capable as the strong type, they generally don't prepare well. They are more casual in their appearance and thus more prone to bad habits such as leaving buttons unbuttoned. Clothes to them are secondary. They analyze well. They tend to put off decisions on even some of the smaller issues, and frequently ask for more supporting data or facts to help make up for their lack of preparation. This tactic also provides them more time to think.

The weak type

These people are very reluctant to move and would much rather have a higher-up make the decisions. They will frequently ask for time to think things over. Their uncertainty often makes them very nervous and subject to numerous bad habits such as fingernail biting and squinting. Both their procrastination and bad habits are good clues to their identity. Their dress runs all over the lot because their uncertainty allows them little time to concentrate on it. In most instances, it's better to bypass these people and go to their higher-up rather than attempt to demonstrate to them and have them convince their superior. In fact, often their superior controls them to such an extent that this type of person will ask for information during the discussion without being able to justify the reason why. That's another good way to spot them. Be patient with them and encourage them, and they will respond as fully as they are able to.[3]

KNOWLEDGE OF YOUR OPPONENT'S MOTIVES IS IMPORTANT

A common event in negotiating occurs when your opponent advances an argument or adopts a posi-

---

3. Adapted from John Ilich, *The Art and Skill of Successful Negotiation* (Englewood Cliffs, N. J.: Prentice-Hall, 1973), pp. 95–97.

tion that is puzzling. The argument just doesn't seem logical or fit in with what you think your opponent should be arguing or adopting. When such a situation occurs, you should immediately ask yourself *why* your opponent is doing it. The answer should reveal your opponent's motives, because motives are what cause people to do what they do.

For example, John was negotiating an important matter and his opponents continually brought up issues that were neither important nor relevant. After considerable reflection of the opponents' motives, John determined that they were really attempting to delay the negotiation. Rather than ask for a delay, which they knew would not be agreed to, they were attempting to stall the process.

Your opponent's puzzling behavior may stem from a variety of reasons such as lack of knowledge, lack of experience, or even the desire to make you angry in order to get you to make admissions that are damaging to your negotiating position. Whatever the case, ask yourself the key question—Why? Once you have discovered your opponent's motives, you are in a good position to counter with strategy and techniques of your own.

MENTAL PRACTICE CAN INCREASE YOUR NEGOTIATING POWER

Proper mental practice will enhance your ability to increase your negotiating power, and can be superior to actual practice. The basic reason is that the subconscious mind and the nervous system cannot distinguish between the experience of actually performing an act and the identical experience conceived in the mind.

Several examples will illustrate the meaning of mental practice. Doris Day, one of America's most popular singers and actresses, polished and perfected her singing and dancing by mental practice:

> I would drag myself home at night, too tired to move another step, but I kept practicing—in my head. . . . I could rehearse a dance routine in my head, watching myself perform, and that did me almost as much good as getting up on my feet and doing it. I rehearsed songs that way too. Not just lyrics, but the actual rendition of the song, the phrasing, breathing, all of it, *without singing a note*. (Emphasis added.)[4]

Josef Hofmann, the renowned concert pianist, represents another example of effectively using mental practice. While on a train bound for a city in which he was to give his next concert, he was leaning back in his seat with his eyes closed. A friend asked, "Are you sleeping?"

"No," replied Hofmann, "I'm practicing."

Hofmann, of course, was doing what Doris Day did, namely, imagining playing the songs and music before his audience.

You, too, will benefit greatly by visualizing yourself negotiating with your opponent, going through

---

4. A. E. Hotchner, *Doris Day* (New York: Morrow, 1976), p. 146.

each phase of the negotiation as if your opponent were actually there before you. And you should, in this regard, even visualize your opponent raising objections to your positions and your response. Mental practice in this manner will sharpen your negotiating skills.

BE IMAGINATIVE, YET NATURAL

Negotiation is normally a free-wheeling affair with no formal rules or guidelines to govern the conduct of the negotiating parties. You can turn this free-wheeling nature to your advantage by adopting negotiating approaches that are different and fresh.

Let your imagination go. Try some new moves. Nothing can put an opponent into quicker and greater disarray than to be exposed to a fresh, imaginative, and unexpected negotiating approach.

But being creative does not mean being unnatural or artificial. When you negotiate, use your own natural style that you are comfortable with. Let your own personality show. Since everyone is different and there are no predetermined methods that can fit all negotiators in all situations, naturalness and directness are the keys to portraying sincerity, which will, in most instances, favorably influence your opponent toward your negotiating objectives.

Naturalness has another important benefit that will aid you in any negotiation. It will free your mind to concentrate on the negotiation rather than on how you are acting.

KEEP COOL, OBJECTIVE, AND UNEMOTIONAL

Good poker players learn to develop a poker face that does not reveal the value of the cards they hold. Facial expressions, tone of voice, and body movements must all remain consistent so that their opponents have no idea what cards they hold.

Objectivity and a certain detachment are also assets to negotiators. Haven't you noticed how much easier it is to negotiate for something less important or for something you have decided you can really live without? That's because your emotions can more easily be kept in check.

Women's emotional sensitivity is often an asset, but in negotiating, feelings should be kept out of sight. One woman described her difficulties in keeping emotions out of her dealings with a man she worked with. "My superior is incompetent," she said. "I really have to work at working with this man. I get angry and stomp out. He can mix personal and business matters and never get upset, but I have a tough time."

Emotional decisions usually turn out to be wrong decisions. If, for example, you become angry and make a decision while angry, your objective reasoning ability is impaired. You may therefore say and do things that you would ordinarily not say or do. The safest route therefore is to work to control your emotions at all times. You can do this with practice. When you feel you are becoming emotional, work to suppress the feeling. If you are still having problems keeping your objectivity, ask for a recess for as long as you think is necessary for you to get back in complete control.

Another helpful practice is to conduct an analysis after every negotiation session. Ask yourself whether the decisions you made during the session were objective or emotional. If your hindsight shows you leaned toward being emotional, resolve that you will not stumble over that same stone twice. With more experience, and with careful analysis of each session, you will find that you are improving your objectivity and that your emotions are in control most of the time, with a corresponding rise in your success rate.

DON'T BE RELUCTANT TO BE ASSERTIVE

Women who conceal their real feelings, wants, and needs and go along with someone else's demands or requests for fear of hurting feelings or to avoid taking a stand are not being assertive. They are being passive.

For example, assume a friend wants to borrow your expensive new camera, which is your pride and joy. You wanted the camera for a long time and you finally saved enough money to buy it. The nonassertive response to your friend would be, "Well, I guess you can borrow it," knowing full well you don't really want to loan it. The assertive response, said in a positive tone, would be "No, I don't want to loan out my new camera. Thank you, however, for your interest."

Don't be reluctant to be assertive when negotiating. Speak up for what you want and, in many instances, you will find that you will get what you want.

GO INTO ANY NEGOTIATION WITH A WINNING ATTITUDE AND BE PERSISTENT

Your personal resolve to succeed in any negotiation will play an important role in whether you succeed. Persistence is so essential to negotiating success that the two are virtually inseparable. There is a story of a gold miner who spent many years digging in the side of a mountain. Eventually, he gave up and moved on. Gold was later discovered by another miner barely one foot beyond where the first miner had stopped digging.

Go that extra foot in every negotiation you engage in, even if your opponent has said no! We have found that with determination and persistence, no is often changed to yes.

A simple secret to tapping your creative mechanism is to evoke the *feeling of success*. When you feel successful, you act successfully and can literally do no wrong.[5] Winners consistently have a winning attitude.

SET OUT TO "WIN" THE NEGOTIATION

Winning in negotiation means accomplishing your negotiating objectives. For example, if you are negotiating the purchase of an asset and have set a target price that you are willing to pay for that asset, successfully negotiating the purchase at or lower than your target price means that you have won that negotiation. You should definitely set out to win any negotiation by setting your nego-

---

5. Maxwell Maltz, *Psycho-Cybernetics* (Englewood Cliffs, N. J.: Prentice-Hall, 1960), p. 225.

tiating objectives and working to accomplish those objectives.

Frequently, some negotiators advocate that there is no such thing as winning a negotiation and that the negotiator should strive to negotiate on the basis that all negotiating parties come away from the negotiation with the attainment of their negotiating objectives. On occasion that may occur. In most instances, however, it will not occur. In the foregoing purchase illustration, for example, your target price may be much lower than the seller's target price for selling the asset. Clearly the seller comes out second best in the negotiation if you are the one who acquired the asset at your target price.

Certainly, if the seller is happy with the final outcome and walks away from the negotiation feeling like a winner, that is an ideal situation and one you should work toward. But if you are faced with the choice of either attaining your negotiating objectives or making your opponent happy, strive to walk away from the negotiation with your negotiating objectives accomplished, which is why you negotiated in the first place.

DON'T BLUFF

Bluffing occurs frequently in negotiation, particularly with inexperienced negotiators. Bluffing is risky because your opponent may call your bluff, forcing you to "prove it or else." The or else means that if you fail to substantiate what you advocate, your credibility will have vanished and you will have lost a considerable amount of negotiating power. Moreover, if you make the further mistake of continuing the practice of bluffing with other negotiating opponents, you will be running the additional risk of developing a reputation as a bluffer.

The best approach, therefore, is to avoid bluffing. Be fully prepared to back up everything you advocate with proof and/or action.

To illustrate, suppose you are settling a dispute and inform your opponent that if settlement is not made within ten days, you are going to sue. If that ten-day period passes and you do not sue, the negotiating momentum has swung to your opponent and it is highly unlikely that you will be able to successfully conclude the negotiation *unless* you are able to give your opponent an acceptable reason why you did not sue as threatened. If you have no reason, your opponent will conclude that you were bluffing all along and will assume that you are bluffing in any further ultimatums.

If, on the other hand, you do file suit after the ten-day period, you can be sure that your opponent will know that you are a negotiator to reckon with and your opponent will treat any of your future ultimatums with respect and consideration. Moreover, you will be developing a solid negotiation reputation, thus greatly facilitating your chances of attaining success in your future negotiations.

TAKE ADVANTAGE OF RECESSES

If at any time during the negotiation you feel that your confidence is seriously faltering or something else is bothering you, tactfully ask for a recess. Few negotiators realize that they can utilize recesses as part of their strategy rather than merely treating them as opportunities to take a break.

The recess you request may be a short one, such as a 15-minute coffee break. Or it may be a longer one, perhaps for a day or more. The point is that you should make recesses your ally in the negotiation and not merely take them for granted or take them only when your opponent suggests them. One good way to control the negotiation is by taking the initiative in suggesting when and how long recesses should be taken. In most instances your opponent will agree.

Use the recess to do more research or preparation or to reinforce your confidence and composure by reviewing and thinking positive thoughts. If you are not able to do this in the time allotted for the recess, contact your opponent and ask for more time.

KEEP YOUR OPTIONS OPEN

Some negotiators get locked into their preliminary goals and expectations and fail to see that more can sometimes be gained by shifting to other goals, inducements, or compromises. There is more than one way to finance a car and more than one way to pay off a debt. Keep all the doors open as long as possible before deciding which one to walk through.

While keeping your own options open, try to close off your opponent's options. As options decrease, so does negotiating power.

AVOID SNAP DECISIONS

Some people appear to be making snap decisions, but in reality they have been carefully preparing for a long time, and they also understand all the ramifications of their decisions. If you have all of the facts and have carefully considered what you want and can get, delay is of no benefit.

Other people, however, make decisions in haste, without adequate preparation, perhaps because they are being pressured by the opponent and fear a delay will further jeopardize their position or perhaps because they panic when presented with new information and want to get the whole process over with.

Rather than making a hasty decision you may later regret, consider either asking for additional time to think it over or if that isn't feasible, saying no. When in doubt, saying no is a far better answer than an uninformed, hasty yes.

CHAPTER 5

Problems to Anticipate and How to Deal with Them

Some of the problems that you may encounter when you negotiate are those confronting almost all negotiators at one time or another. Other problems may be unique to you. Whichever the case, you can react in either of two ways. You can allow the problems to defeat you or you can work to overcome them.

THE PROBLEM OF UNDERESTIMATION

Underestimation in negotiation is a common occurrence and can arise because of a variety of reasons or a combination of reasons such as your age, appearance, education level, or educational or ethnic background. Older negotiators, for example, frequently feel that they are wiser and more competent than younger negotiators solely because of age and therefore are prone to underestimating younger negotiators.

You may be faced with an opponent, either male or female, who feels superior to you simply because you are a woman.

Although your natural reaction to having your ability underestimated may be anger or frustration, you can, in fact, use your opponent's underestimation to your advantage. Chances are good that any opponent who is underestimating your ability will be prone to letting his or her guard down; that is, relaxing both during preparation for and during the actual negotiation. In sporting events, for example, a heavily favored team may let its guard down to such an extent that the underdog wins the contest. You can therefore see the unique opportunity these underestimation situations give you if you maintain the right attitude.

You should press that much harder to attain your negotiating objectives. You can be sure that your opponents, once they discover that you are quite capable, will scurry to recover. Often, however, it is too late and your opponents' underestimation is a major factor in your attainment of your negotiating objectives.

THE PROBLEM OF TIMIDITY

Timidity can also occur from a variety of causes or combination of causes. Perhaps you are new at negotiating and, in addition, are inhibited because you are self-conscious about trying to exert power for the first time. Perhaps you have tried to negotiate in the past but were not successful. Whatever the reason, set out to eliminate your lack of confidence, which can be done in a number of ways.

Overcoming Your Timidity by Eliminating Your Fears

Fear of the unknown and fear of failure are two familiar culprits that will work to keep you timid. Fear of the unknown occurs because you can't foresee exactly what lies ahead of you when you get into the actual negotiation. Your mind may conjure up all kinds of drastic events, such as your opponent is an expert who will bowl you over, or that you may be embarrassed because of your lack of experience. You must put this kind of thinking out of your mind so that you are free to concentrate on preparing for the negotiation and on the actual negotiation itself. Otherwise you will be severely handicapped.

Thomas Jefferson put it best when he said, "How much pain the evils have cost us that have never happened." You will find that most, if not all, of your fears of the unknown will never happen. And even if they do, they are usually not as painful as you imagined. So don't dwell on or even acknowledge those fears. Sweep them away by replacing them with other, more positive thoughts or by concentrating on your preparation and execution so that there is no idle time to allow your fears to reenter your thinking.

The same is true of fear of failure. If you allow it, fear of failure can become so intense you may be literally programming yourself to fail. Eliminate the fear by replacing it with positive thoughts of success and by concentrating on your preparation and execution.

Overcoming Timidity by Sound Preparation

Preparing thoroughly will go a long way toward eliminating timidity. The method you use to prepare should be one that works best for you. Adopt a method that is systematic and thorough and one that can be used in virtually any negotiation you undertake, large or small, simple or complex.

The method John has devised is called the *Stick Theory* and enables him to prepare quickly and thoroughly for almost any negotiation. His system also enables him to go confidently into the negotiation with the knowledge that everything relevant to the negotiation is right at his fingertips. The premise of John's method is that there are only so many areas that need to be researched and analyzed in each negotiation and there is no need to load yourself down with unnecessary data.

Take buying a car, for example. The only relevant factors are the gross price (including extras), the trade-in value of your present car, the financial terms if you want to finance, and the quality and availability of service after the sale. If you have researched and analyzed these areas in advance and know what you are after, you are well prepared.[1]

If you follow a specific preparation scheme that you are comfortable with; that enables you to organize quickly and efficiently, your mind will be free to concentrate on the negotiation. This freedom will make you a more effective negotiator than if

---

1. See John Ilich, *The Art and Skill of Successful Negotiation* (Englewood Cliffs, N.J.: Prentice-Hall, 1973), pp. 39–42.

you were forced to draw away your precious concentration in order to assimilate data or even attempt to locate documents or other information that you may need during the negotiation.

Moreover, it is always impressive and, to a great extent, even demoralizing to your opponent to see you effortlessly produce a document or other data without even a break in your concentration or in what you are saying. This ease of delivery increases your negotiating power because it has the effect of placing your opponent on the defensive. Your opponent's reasoning might go something like this: "The way she came up with that document means that she obviously knows what she is doing. Maybe her position is correct."

Overcoming Timidity by Gaining Experience

Experience is another important way to overcome timidity. After each negotiation, your confidence will grow, and as you gain confidence your timidity will, in turn, diminish and eventually disappear.

In addition to actually participating in a variety of negotiations, experience can be gained by reading. Books and articles are truly the *wings of wisdom*. You should take every opportunity to read, especially material that deals with people—psychology and history. Since negotiation is essentially mind pitted against mind, reading anything that deals with the human mind can be only beneficial to you and your development.

Other Techniques to Help You Overcome Timidity

To help bolster your confidence, especially during the initial stages of the negotiation when your fears are apt to be the greatest, you can learn to develop a good lead-in to get you past the difficult starting point. Professional athletes and performers of all kinds, no matter how experienced they are, will tell you that they are nervous and tense until the game or performance starts. Once the action begins, however, nervousness and tenseness disappear and they are free to concentrate on the business at hand.

The same thing will happen to you in most negotiations. The butterflies in the stomach and the cotton in the mouth will lessen and probably go away entirely once the negotiating has begun. Hence, you need to develop a way to get past that roughest period at the beginning with a greater degree of confidence.

Questions are excellent lead-ins because they give you control and place your opponent on the defensive. While your opponent is answering a question, she or he has less time to think of strategies and techniques to use against you. Moreover, by asking a question, you have provided yourself an opportunity to speak and once you have spoken those first words, your timidity will have substantially diminished.

The question you ask can take any form. You might ask your opponent, for instance, for information such as, "Do you have a copy of the deed?" Or maybe your question is directed toward substantiating a fact, such as, "Is your letter to Mrs. Johnson dated March 23rd?" Your question should, of course, be relevant to the negotiation and be of sufficient substance that your opponent will not suspect that you are asking the question primarily to bolster your own confidence and to get you by the critical opening stage.

Have some questions ready to ask as a means of getting past starting point jitters in the event you deem it necessary when the negotiation begins.

HOW TO DEAL WITH DELIBERATE ATTEMPTS TO INTIMIDATE YOU

There are numerous reasons why your opponent may attempt to intimidate you. Your opponent, for instance, may be a bully. Your opponent may be doing it as a matter of deliberate negotiating strategy in order to put you on the defensive. Your opponent may feel that he or she has the superior negotiating position and is in no mood to compromise.

Whatever the reason, the best way to counter deliberate intimidation attempts is to confront them right at the time they are made. If, for example, you sense that your opponent is a bully, you can easily counter by not backing away from your opponent's intimidation attempts but firmly and tactfully (you don't want to stifle negotiation progress) maintaining your negotiating position. If you sense your opponent is attempting to intimidate you as a matter of negotiation strategy, here again, firmly but tactfully maintain your negotiating position. This stance will tell your opponent that you do not intend to be intimidated.

An opponent who is attempting to intimidate you because he feels his position is superior ordinarily will quickly back down when you display a firm and tactful position.

THE PROBLEM OF MAKING LARGE, INITIAL CONCESSIONS

Negotiators who make large, initial concessions normally come out second best because such large concessions made early swing the negotiating momentum to the opponent, thereby giving the opponent more confidence and making the opponent less likely to make similar concessions. By making large, initial concessions the negotiator appears weak in the opponent's eyes even though that may not be the true situation. The ultimate impact is to considerably lessen the negotiator's power.

The best way to avoid having to make large, initial concessions is to be certain that all of your positions and arguments can be substantiated by solid factual or legal support or by expert opinion. When your opponent attacks your positions, you have the supporting material to back them up. This approach tells your opponent that your positions are based upon solid support and are therefore valid and should be agreed to by your opponent.

For example, assume you are negotiating the purchase of a real estate parcel for which you offer $2,000 per acre. Your objective is to acquire the property for $2,500 to $2,800 per acre. You are willing to go as high as $2,800 because you really want the property. Your opponent, of course, is unaware of your great desire.

Your opponent thinks the property is worth at least $4,000 per acre and therefore thinks you purposely made your initial offer low and are really shooting for a final price of around $3,500 per acre. If, in response to your opponent's stated price of $4,000 per acre, you immediately increase your offer to $2,800, that is a large, initial concession that will give the momentum to your opponent and deprive you of considerable power. Chances are slim that you will acquire the property for the $2,800 top price you have set as your objective.

If, on the other hand, you have solid factual data to support your initial $2,000 per acre offering price, you could use that data to support your initial offer. Perhaps you have evidence that a similar piece of property nearby recently sold for $2,000 per acre. Or maybe you have an appraisal from an experienced and knowledgeable individual who concludes that the property is worth about $2,000 per acre. Such opinions can carry great weight, often more weight than they should, and would be sufficient basis for your initial offer of $2,000.

Supporting your offer by such factual or opinion data will not only bolster the substance of your initial $2,000 offer but also place your opponent on the defensive and thus make it highly likely that your opponent will be making a large, initial concession by dropping the asking price. Once your opponent makes such a concession, chances are good that you will be able to ultimately acquire the property for the price you have set as your objective, namely, $2,800 per acre or less.

WHAT TO DO WHEN LARGE, INITIAL CONCESSIONS BECOME NECESSARY

Occasionally, even experienced negotiators are forced to make large, initial concessions. When forced into this conceding posture, the important point to remember is to be certain that the concessions do not transfer negotiating momentum to your opponent. The best way to avoid such a loss of momentum is to be certain that the reason for making any concession is fully explained prior to making it so your opponent does not get the impression that the concession is made because of weakness or lack of confidence on your part.

In addition, large, initial concessions should be made on a something-for-something basis whenever possible. You say, in essence, "Okay, I'll concede on this if you make this concession." Any large, initial concession is thus traded for a concession from your opponent and the danger of the momentum shifting to your opponent is therefore greatly minimized.

To further illustrate, in the above real estate example, assume that a sale of a similar parcel of property sold a short period prior to the negotiation for $3,000 per acre. You know that your opponent will undoubtedly be aware of this sale so you decide to increase your offer to $2,500 per acre because, as previously related, you really want the property. You therefore inform your opponent that your basis for increasing your offer from $2,000 to $2,500 is the sale of the other property for $3,000 per acre and that you are not going as high as $3,000 per acre because you feel the land you are negotiating for is not precisely of the same high quality as the land that sold for $3,000 per acre.

This approach has a twofold effect. First, it establishes a valid reason for your concession so that it doesn't make it appear that you are dealing with arbitrary values, thus alleviating to some extent the transfer of negotiating momentum to your opponent. Second, by relating the other land sale rather than allowing your opponent to disclose the information, you have played one of your opponent's aces and have also prevented the momentum from swinging decisively to your opponent.

THE PROBLEM OF DEALING WITH NEGOTIATING MISTAKES

Everyone makes mistakes, including even the most experienced negotiators. Negotiating mistakes usually result in a loss of negotiating power because they act as a brake on the favorable momentum you have established.

Learn to Recognize Mistakes Early

Early detection of negotiating mistakes is as important as the early discovery of mistakes in other walks of life. Take fire, for example. Statistics show that the first few minutes are the most vital in saving lives and property. Early detection and warning allow quicker remedial action.

Similarly, the sooner you are aware of a negotiating mistake, the sooner you can take action to either correct the mistake or acknowledge it and move on.

Mistakes of Fact

Assume the negotiation involves the purchase of investment property and you have mistakenly advised your opponent that a similar type of property across the street from the property you are attempting to purchase sold for $250,000 when, in fact, the sales price was $350,000. If your opponent discovers the error, it will reflect adversely on your credibility and dissipate your negotiating power. Your opponent will not be favorably motivated toward your objectives if your opponent feels you are giving out erroneous information. This type of factual error can be especially harmful if it occurs late in the negotiation when matters are well along toward a successful conclusion because your opponent may be concerned about the accuracy of the other information you supplied.

If, on the other hand, you discover your error early in the negotiation and promptly advise your opponent of the error and what the correct factual information actually is, chances are good that your credibility will not be damaged and could actually be enhanced by the disclosure.

The Problem of Facts Distinguished from Hearsay

A common error is failure of the negotiator to get either complete or accurate facts about the subject matter of the negotiation. Positions advocated or advanced by a negotiator that are based upon incomplete or inaccurate facts can only be faulty positions that can, once their fault is exposed, quickly switch the negotiating momentum to the opponent and make it difficult for a negotiator to regain the momentum.

To illustrate the importance of getting complete as well as accurate facts, many years ago when John was beginning his negotiating career, he was involved in negotiating the value of a gasoline service station. He had fully analyzed the station's profit and loss statement and balance sheet as well as an appraisal of the physical structure and land. But one essential fact was lacking. It seemed that the business was located in an area that was quickly deteriorating and several gasoline stations there had already gone out of business. As a consequence, in spite of favorable financial statements and the appraisal, it was clear that future prospects for the business were not bright and any value arrived at had to take that into consideration. From that point on, John made it a set policy whenever possible to visit the actual business site in order to have a complete and accurate factual picture.

This policy quickly paid dividends. Soon thereafter John was involved in the valuation of a business that was earning substantial profits from manufacturing a highly sought-after product. Under these conditions, the business would normally have a high value. But upon visiting the plant, John discovered that both the building and the equipment were so deteriorated that it would take millions of dollars to bring them up to par. The business owners had neglected the building and equipment in order to maximize profits. Future profits, of course, would be substantially lessened in order to pay for or service the debt necessary to bring the plant and equipment back up to a new or dependable condition.

What Is Hearsay?

Hearsay is information not acquired from personal knowledge, but from what has been heard from others. It is second-hand information and therefore more susceptible to inaccuracy or distortion.

You will undoubtedly be exposed to large doses of hearsay, almost all of which will be labeled factual. Some of it *may* be accurate and useful. Much of it, however, will be inaccurate or incomplete and therefore potentially detrimental if you rely on it or use it in the negotiation. In your quest for facts, be certain to distinguish between what is accurate (because it has been substantiated) and what is inaccurate hearsay. There is no quicker way to severely damage your credibility than to discover, perhaps from your opponent, that the hearsay you have been relying upon is inaccurate.

THE PROBLEM OF DEALING WITH AN OLD-FASHIONED MALE

Some men, particularly older ones who were conditioned to believe that a woman's place is in the home, may give you problems. An attractive woman told Barbara that her greatest difficulty was that her male opponents always took on the father role. She felt she was in a double bind because if she allowed herself to be patronized, she was locked into a subservient role but if she fought the stereotype she was putting up extra barriers for herself.

Other women complained that male opponents sometimes tried to mix socializing and business, asking them for dates or trying to make passes. This gave them another double bind because they seemed to lose the round whether they accepted or not.

The best way to handle these situations, although it can be uncomfortable at first, is to be yourself. If you do not like being treated like a daughter, say so in firm, but not hostile, terms and make sure your own behavior does not encourage your male opponent to be fatherly. The best advice on mixing socializing and business is *don't!* One woman explains how she handles this problem. "When clients or business colleagues want to get too friendly and talk about getting together outside of business, I talk about my husband a lot. I explain how happy I am with my husband. When the problem came up before I was married, I was always engaged or had a boy friend who wouldn't like my going out with anyone else."

CHAPTER 6

Personal versus Professional Negotiating: Is There Any Difference?

The question frequently arises as to whether there are any major differences between negotiating a personal matter on your own behalf and negotiating a business matter for a client or for someone other than yourself. Does it, for example, call for a different negotiating approach when negotiating with a contractor for remodeling your home as opposed to a contract for the construction of an addition to a business building? If the answer is yes, then it is important to be fully aware of any differences in order to plan more effectively for and engage in the actual negotiation.

MAJOR COMMON DENOMINATORS

Both Kinds of Negotiation Involve People

The first obvious similarity between personal and business negotiations is that both are conducted by and for people, which insures that there will be close likenesses between conducting personal and business negotiations. Although people react differently, you can usually count on the same basic behavior in similar circumstances.

You need, however, to be alert to the differences in degree. For instance, everyone is capable of becoming angry but each of us angers to different intensities and for different reasons. If a negotiator, for example, uses rough or abusive language toward an opponent, it may make that opponent angry. Yet using the same rough or abusive language toward a different opponent under virtually identical negotiating circumstances may not even draw a reaction.

Your Opponents May Even Be Identical

It is not unusual for negotiating parties to engage in both business and personal negotiations. In the foregoing illustration, for instance, you might be negotiating with the contractor for the construction of an addition to your business building and, during the course of the negotiation, learn that the contractor also remodels homes. You know the contractor has a good reputation for high-quality work, so after the business is completed, you engage in negotiations with the same contractor to do some remodeling of your home.

Similar Subject Matters

In the above example, both are contracts for construction work. The only substantive difference is that one is a contract for personal work and the other for work for a business.

Similar subject matters are common and may involve such diverse matters as settlement of disputes, the sale or purchase of real estate or personal property, and even dealing in unique objects such as jewelry or works of art.

Place of Negotiation

Another major common denominator may be the place of the negotiation and the negotiating physical environment. You may, for example, conduct the negotiations for both a personal contract and a business contract at your business office. Perhaps the personal negotiation is conducted during your lunch period or even after business hours. One negotiation might even directly follow the other with your not really having to move out of your chair.

MAJOR DIFFERENCE

There is one important major difference between negotiating a personal matter for yourself and negotiating professionally for someone else. A person conducting personal negotiations will be much more prone to becoming emotional and, as we have said, emotional tendencies can often be the difference between success and failure.

It is important to keep this major difference firmly fixed in your thinking as you negotiate so that you do not fall victim if you are negotiating on your own behalf and can take advantage of it when your opponent is negotiating personal matters.

Professional women generally agree that it is easier to represent someone else. "I enjoy negotiating and feel good about it as long as I treat it as a game," said a commercial marketing manager. "But I'm least effective and most uncomfortable when negotiating around my own personal needs."

A saleswoman put it this way: "I do better in the field with people I don't know. I'm at ease selling a service or a product because I know more than the customers do and they need the information. But when I come back to the office and negotiate with my supervisor about my personal future, I am apt to fall apart and get stepped on."

Negotiating on Your Own Behalf

When you are negotiating for yourself you will often, usually unintentionally, by your words and actions, send out a clear signal to your opponent that you are personally involved. Your opponent may therefore anticipate that you will allow your emotions to influence your negotiating decisions and may work to heighten that possibility.

To illustrate, assume you are negotiating the purchase of an antique chair that you want for your living room. During the course of the negotiation you relate to your opponent, the chair owner, that you think the chair will "fit beautifully" into your living room. That simple statement has alerted your opponent to the fact that (1) you are conducting the negotiation for yourself, and (2) you are strongly attracted to the chair and will therefore be inclined to be much more disturbed if you cannot acquire it than if you were negotiating for someone else. Your opponent can now, as a consequence of your disclosure, proceed as a matter of strategy to introduce elements into the negotiation that will have a strong tendency to influence you to pay a higher price.

"There is another person who is greatly interested in the chair and will be out in a few hours to talk with me about it," is an illustration of a deliberate strategy to play upon and enhance your fear of losing the chair and to thus motivate you to react emotionally and pay a higher price.

If, on the other hand, you did not tip your hand that you were seeking the chair for yourself, you have *potentially* insulated yourself from your opponent's strategy of playing on your emotions and thus deprived your opponent of negotiating power. Emphasis is placed on the word *potentially* because skilled negotiators will always attempt to learn whether you are conducting the business for yourself or for someone else. They can do this in a variety of ways such as directly asking you if you want the item for yourself or indirectly commenting on how the chair would enhance the decor of any house, and then paying close attention to your response or any reaction, possibly from your facial expression, that would indicate that you want the chair for yourself.

A good tip-off that a person is negotiating on her or his own behalf is overuse of the pronoun, *I*. Take the previous chair example. If you frequently make such comments as "*I* like the style," or "*I* think the price is too high," it tends to indicate that you are negotiating for yourself and a skilled opponent will explore further in an attempt to substantiate that fact.

The Best Approach When Negotiating on Your Own Behalf

As with other negotiations, personal negotiations call for an approach that is objective and neutral in both words and actions, a certain detachment from the subject matter of the negotiation. You need to visualize the subject matter as separate from yourself. Don't telegraph that you so strongly want the item that you can already picture yourself, psychologically, as its owner. Once you acquire an object, even mentally, it becomes a part of you.

Your goal, then, is to remain detached from the object of the negotiation to such an extent that even if your opponent is a skilled negotiator and is attempting to learn whether you are negotiating on your own behalf, nothing you say or do will supply the answer. It takes practice to assume this role, but once you have mastered it you have virtually eliminated the major difference between the two types of negotiation and are thus on your way to becoming a much more effective negotiator irrespective of whether you are negotiating for yourself or for another.

The Best Approach to Take When Your Opponent Is Negotiating on Her or His Own Behalf

When your opponent is negotiating a personal matter, the situation is reversed. Your opponent may be the one prone to becoming emotional and making decisions on an emotional basis because of fear of losing the subject matter of the negotiation. As early as possible, probe to find out on whose behalf your opponent is negotiating. Also probe until you learn how strongly attached to the subject matter your opponent is and whether your opponent is likely to be motivated by such factors as fear of loss.

For example, in the chair illustration, assume your opponent says, "I want it for a relative. I owe the relative a gift." If you are convinced that the statements are genuine, you can reasonably conclude that your opponent is not likely to fear losing the chair because it is being bought to satisfy an obligation and your opponent may not care whether the obligation is satisfied by purchasing the chair or something else. Unless something turns up later in the negotiation to lead you to conclude otherwise, avoid any strategy centering around your opponent's negotiating personally for herself or himself.

Watch for Opponents Who Try to Mislead You About Their Motives

An important assumption in the preceding example was that you were convinced that your opponent's expressed motive for purchasing the chair for a relative to satisfy an obligation was genuine. On occasion, however, you will encounter opponents who deliberately attempt to mislead you about their motives.

If, in the chair example, you detected that your opponent's expressed motive was not genuine and was merely a ploy to hide the fact that your opponent really wanted the chair personally, you could reasonably conclude that your opponent wanted that chair very badly. Additional probing should help you verify your conclusion and enable you to use that information to your own great advantage.

CHAPTER 7

How to Make the Offer or Counteroffer

The technique to be used when making the offer varies, depending upon whether you are buying or selling and depending upon whether the buyer or seller has initiated the transaction. The nature of the property, for the most part, whether real estate or personal property, seldom plays a significant role in the technique used because it is still people who will be conducting the negotiations, and human minds are fairly constant.

In most cases, your negotiating opponent's emotional attachment to the property shouldn't materially influence your offer. To illustrate, assume the owner of a house decides to sell without the services of a real estate broker, which is a frequent occurrence. Assume the owner has retired and intends to move to a warmer climate or is required to move because of health or other reasons. Assume that the owner has lived in the house for a sufficient number of years to become strongly attached to the property from an emotional standpoint. This emotional attachment will influence the owner to set a higher price than might otherwise be the case. Nevertheless, the final impact of that influence might be negligible. If you have done the necessary homework, you will discover that the house is overpriced and will make an offer that more truly reflects the real market value.

In situations like these where the seller has set too high a sales price, the property will frequently remain unsold for a long period of time, or be taken off the market because it cannot be sold at the inflated offering price, or the property will later be listed for sale with a real estate broker at a lower price. If the seller leaves the property on the market at the inflated price, the sheer passage of time will decrease the seller's negotiating leverage because a knowledgeable buyer will know that the price set by the seller failed to attract any buyers. The buyer will therefore feel comfortable in making an even lower offer than the buyer may have originally anticipated with a greater likelihood that the buyer will eventually acquire the property for a good price, especially if the seller is anxious to sell and the buyer is aware of the anxiety.

MAKING THE OFFER WHEN THE BUYER INITIATES THE PURCHASE NEGOTIATIONS

Buyers frequently seek out property to purchase. In the typical situation, the buyer approaches the property owner (hereinafter called the seller), expresses an interest in purchasing the property and asks the seller, "How much do you want for the property?" or similar language that is designed to get the seller to quote a sales price. How should the seller respond? Should the seller give a price or decline to?

In most cases, if you are the seller you should neither give a price nor decline to. If you respond to the buyer's inquiry by giving a price, you have set the highest amount that you can expert to receive for the property. Moreover, you have provided the buyer with an opportunity to use your quoted price as a starting point from which the buyer can negotiate a lower price. If, on the other hand, you decline to give a price you may run the risk of either antagonizing the buyer and thus stifling negotiation progress or turning the buyer completely off, thus losing an opportunity to sell the property.

The best approach is for you to attempt to get the buyer to open the process with an offer on the property. This can provide you with an opportunity to potentially get a price even higher than you would ordinarily ask; in addition, you can start the bargaining at the price set by the buyer if you deem the buyer's initial offer to be too low.

To illustrate the great advantage that can often be obtained from allowing the buyer to make the initial offer, consider the experience of James Ling, chief builder of L.T.V. Corporation, a large, multinational company. Ling expected the opening bid on a company he was selling to be in the area of $60 to $65 million dollars. But Ling wisely allowed the buyer to make the initial offer, which turned out to be $90 million—$25 to $30 million higher than what Ling expected. If Ling had led with a $60 to $65 million offer, he would have set a ceiling on what he could have expected to receive. Simply allowing the buyer to make the first offer resulted in Ling's receiving an opening offer of $25 to $30 million higher than anticipated.[1]

HOW TO GET THE BUYER TO MAKE THE INITIAL OFFER

When a buyer has expressed an interest in the property it usually is not too difficult to get that person to make the initial offer. When asked by the buyer what price you are willing to sell the property for, simply reply, "Make me an offer."

If that doesn't work and the buyer counters by confessing ignorance of the property's worth (this "confession" of ignorance of the property's worth is often a favorite tactic of skilled negotiators who want to get sellers to commit themselves) you might easily counter by advising the buyer that you are really not too interested in selling, but

---

1. Stanley Brown, *Ling: The Rise and Fall of a Texas Titan* (New York: Atheneum, 1972), p. 229.

will entertain any realistic offer that the buyer may make. This action quickly switches the burden of making the initial offer back to the buyer.

Another strategy is to say to the buyer who wants to know your price, "You said you wanted to buy. I didn't say I wanted to sell."[2] The essential point is that whatever language you use, you merely indicate to the buyer that it is the buyer who should make the initial offer since the buyer is the one who initiated the negotiation. This approach normally will not alienate or antagonize the buyer or force the buyer to break off negotiations since the buyer is aware (or should be) that the person who initiates the negotiation should be prepared to make the first offer.

DON'T BE TOO ANXIOUS WHEN MAKING YOUR OFFER

Very often in negotiation one or sometimes both sides become anxious about making an offer, whether the subject matter is the sale of an asset or the settling of a dispute. Offers made with obviously anxious overtones are tip-offs to your opponent that you possess a great desire to either buy or sell (as the case may be) the asset or settle the dispute as quickly as possible. Skilled negotiators look for such tip-offs that place you at a definite negotiating disadvantage because your opponent may convert your anxiety into negotiating power

2. John Ilich, *The Art and Skill of Successful Negotiation* (Englewood Cliffs, N.J.: Prentice-Hall, 1973), p. 169.

by making you fear losing the purchase or sale or settling the dispute. Your opponent can do this by indicating a lack of interest in your offer. The result may cause you to increase your offer if you are the buyer, decrease the price if you are the seller, or settle the dispute for a lesser sum than would ordinarily be the case.

BEWARE OF QUESTIONS

In the process of making offers and counteroffers, questions will undoubtedly be asked and answered by both sides. As previously discussed, a simple question is one of the most effective tools used to gain information from a negotiating opponent. Some questions, however, are not as simple as they appear.

For example, assume the negotiation involves the purchase of a house. With the seller present, the prospective buyer inspects the property with the seller's broker. The buyer is interested in discovering whether there is an immediate need for the seller to make the sale, because if such a need exists, there is a good possibility that the seller will be anxious to sell and therefore more receptive to accepting a much lower price. The buyer has learned from the broker that the seller will be moving out of the city, so during the inspection the buyer casually asks the seller, "When are you leaving the city?" Although this might seem like a harmless question, notice that the buyer asked *when* and not *why*. The question, "Why are you leaving?" is too general and also too obvious to be effective.

Most sellers will have a pat answer ready to

indicate a reason for selling other than a real need to sell. "I am considering moving to a warmer climate," is a typical response, with "considering" being the key word to make it appear that there is no pressure to move. By specifically directing the question to when the seller is going to move, however, the buyer has adeptly attempted to learn whether the move must be made soon and thus whether pressure to sell exists. Certainly, the seller could have answered, "I am considering moving" but often when confronted with a specific question, such as when they are moving, people will give you the moving date or some other specific information. And it is not unusual to have the person tie in the time for making the move to the sale of the house by saying something like, "I hope to move as soon as I can get the house sold." Once that type of disclosure has been made, the buyer has ample ammunition to come in with a lower offer.

So beware of questions, especially questions that are specific and damaging to your negotiating position. It is surprising how often people feel compelled to answer all questions put to them as if they were on a witness stand, even when the answer may be damaging to their best interests. In employment interviews, for example, women are often asked questions about their marital status or family plans, which are irrelevant to the job. But women feel pressured to answer these questions for fear the prospective employer will think them evasive or uncooperative. But their very willingness to answer the questions puts them in a weakened negotiating position.

SET A TIME LIMIT ON ANY OFFER

Time limits are necessary for a number of important reasons. First, a great number of offers are accepted at or near the deadline. As the time limit for acceptance of the offer approaches, the person faced with the decision normally begins to experience uneasiness and considers what will be lost if the offer is not accepted.

Another aspect to remember is that the time limit, particularly if it is short, will work to prevent your opponent from shopping around for higher offers and, if some can be found, either accepting them or coming back to you to seek an even higher offer from you. So keep the time limit short. Depending on the nature of the negotiation, the time limit can vary from as little as a few hours to several days or a week. It is seldom wise to set the limit beyond a week, especially when the sale or purchase of real estate or personal property is involved.

Finally, setting a deadline for acceptance of any offers helps you to formulate your own plans. Contrast that to a situation where no deadline has been set and you have no idea when you might hear from your opponent on whether your offer has been accepted or rejected.

WHEN SHOULD YOU EXTEND A TIME LIMIT?

The reputation you are striving to develop in negotiation is that you say what you mean and mean what you say. When you put a time limit on the period in which your offer can be accepted, you should be fully prepared to accept the consequences if the offer is not accepted within that time limit. You should not arbitrarily extend the time for acceptance of the offer without a justifiable reason. If you extend the time without a good reason, your opponent may not take your time limits seriously now or in the future. In addition, you run the risk of developing a reputation as a willing time-limit extender.

Don't hesitate to extend the time limit if you feel there is justification for doing so. But be certain you fully explain the basis for the extension to your opponent so he or she doesn't construe the extension as a sign of weakness on your part.

USE DIRECT EYE CONTACT WHEN YOU MAKE YOUR OFFER

As previously related, one of the best methods to convey an attitude of confidence is to look your opponent right in the eyes. This is especially important when you are making the offer. Too often, negotiators look away from their opponents at the critical time when they are making an offer. This leaves their opponents with an impression that the negotiator either lacks confidence or sincerity with the offer even though that may not be the case at all.

Make no mistake about it, reaching the offering stage is a critical stage in negotiations because it is then that you are saying, "This is what I think is the worth of the subject matter of this negotiation." When you make that statement, you are putting yourself on the line as being sincere and believing in your offer. It is therefore essential that you convey an attitude of sincerity and confidence. Making direct eye contact is a good method to accomplish this important objective.

BE FULLY PREPARED FOR ANY REACTION AFTER YOU MAKE YOUR OFFER

Your opponent's reaction to your offer is often difficult to predict. The fact that you feel your offer is fair and reasonable does not necessarily mean your opponent will feel the same way. On the contrary, your opponent may perceive your offer as wholly unrealistic and inadequate and may do anything from laugh in your face to call you names. Be prepared for a wide variety of possible reactions and remain absolutely calm. Even if your opponent's reaction is drastic, do not become angry. If you do, you will be dissipating your own negotiating power. As we have said before, anger is an emotional response and your emotions should be left out of the negotiation.

Instead, take the offensive and immediately and calmly ask your opponent to explain the negative reaction. Don't let the opponent regain the offensive by answering your question with a question. If, for example, you ask your opponent, "Why do you think my offer is unreasonable?" do not allow your opponent to counter with a question such as, "Why do you feel your offer is reasonable?" You are placed on the defensive if you attempt to answer such a question and, as we all know, it is not the defense that scores points but the offense.

So you might counter your opponent's question with another question of your own: "I gave you a full explanation of the basis for my offer but is there any part you want me to amplify?" Here again, your object is to get your opponent to explain why he or she feels your offer is unreasonable. Once that explanation has been given, you then have an opportunity to counter with a further explanation of your own and thus maintain the momentum for negotiation progress and acceptance of your offer.

But if your opponent's objections to your offer appear to be genuine and you have no more information with which to counter, do not hesitate to either adjust your offer or to ask for more time to consider the objections. It is unwise, when you perceive that your opponent's objections to your offer are genuine, to persist to attempt to persuade your opponent that your offer is fair and reasonable. By taking such an approach you run a great risk of a complete breakdown in communication with your opponent because your opponent will probably become unreceptive to what you are advocating.

BE CERTAIN TO DOCUMENT ORAL OFFERS

Offers are frequently made orally, particularly when the subject matter involves personal property or the settlement of a dispute. When this occurs, there is a danger that the precise terms and conditions of your offer may be misunderstood or forgotten over time. That's why it is best to submit your offer in writing whenever possible. If it isn't possible, document your oral offer by such means as a written memorandum or your personal notes. Suggest and encourage your opponent to record your offer and compare that record with yours to be sure that both are the same. This procedure helps to avoid later misunderstandings about the terms.

If your opponent is not prepared to record the terms and conditions of your oral offer, jot them down yourself and give your opponent a copy. Don't be shy about insisting on a record. Be tactful, considerate and, above all, bold.

HOW TO REACT TO YOUR OPPONENT'S OFFER

Listen carefully to your opponent's offer and make direct eye contact while the offer is being made. This will enable you to accomplish two objectives. First, it will help insure that you clearly understand all the terms and conditions. Second, your careful observation will provide you with clues about your opponent's sincerity and confidence in the offer. If the opponent looks away from your eye contact, a lack of confidence and/or sincerity may be reasons. You can test that possibility by raising reasons why you feel the offer is unacceptable. If your opponent's response is to alter the offer, chances are good that the opponent had little faith in the original offer and fully expected to alter it.

If your opponent's offer is oral, record it, preferably right after the offer is made; read your recorded notes aloud and get your opponent's concurrence on the accuracy of your recording. This insures that both you and your opponent are in complete agreement on the terms and conditions of the offer and should avoid any later misunderstanding.

WEIGH YOUR OPPONENT'S OFFER IN LIGHT OF FUTURE DEVELOPMENTS

This consideration is one of the most overlooked and neglected aspects of negotiation, and frequently results in the rejection of offers that should be accepted. For example, John was negotiating the purchase of a large parcel of real estate for a client. The seller offered the property for a price that was about 20 percent higher than the market value. Making a counteroffer for at least 20 percent less would have clearly been warranted. John made a counteroffer, however, *accepting* the seller's price, but on a square foot basis on only a small part of the property with the option to buy the balance as needed on the same square foot basis. Since John's client's initial square footage need was small, only a small initial cash payment was required. As time wore on and inflation continued to cause the value of the property to substantially increase, the original offering price proposed by the seller and accepted by the buyer would be a bargain by the time John's client needed and was required to purchase the rest of the property.

DO NOT OVERLOOK COUNTEROFFERS

A counteroffer is a variation of an offer and a rejection of the offer. A counteroffer is thus a new offer.

It is surprising how often negotiators fail to take advantage of counteroffers. One negotiating side will make an offer and the other side will either accept or reject it instead of proposing a modification. The net effect is often substantial loss of negotiating power since a successful offer and acceptance can often be concluded with only a variation on the original offer.

There are important advantages in making a counteroffer. One advantage is that a counteroffer facilitates negotiation progress because it is frequently not a complete alteration but only a slight modification. By accepting part of your opponent's offer, you have made negotiating progress.

Another advantage of making counteroffers is that it gives you the opportunity to put forth what *you* feel are acceptable terms and conditions. You then have greater negotiating control because your terms and conditions are placed on the table with your counteroffer and your opponent must either accept them or reject them. If your opponent accepts them you have undoubtedly attained your objectives. If your opponent accepts part of them and rejects part of them, you have still made important progress. Even if your opponent rejects all of them, you still have the option of asking your opponent to make a new offer or to make a new offer of your own. So even in this latter situation, you have not lost any appreciable ground by making your counteroffer.

Consider a counteroffer in virtually every negotiation and make one whenever it is in your best interests. Do not feel limited to either accepting or rejecting your opponent's offers as so many negotiators unwisely do.

CHAPTER 8

Negotiating a Raise in Pay

Asking the boss for a raise is something most of us have to do from time to time. Some of us succeed in getting those extra dollars. Many fail. Fortunately, the cause of failure can be remedied in most instances because the cause is not within the boss (although the boss usually gets the blame) but within the person seeking a raise.

THE MAJOR CAUSES OF FAILURE AND HOW TO REMEDY THEM

Fear of Loss

Fear of loss is one of the two major reasons why most raise seekers fail. We fear, quite simply, that we will lose our job—that the boss will see us as getting out of line and will fire us either immediately or soon thereafter. This fear is our unwelcome companion as we sit or stand before our superior. This fear often forces our voices to falter and our bodies to assume a defensive physical posture. Perhaps we unconsciously take on sub-missive behavior and don't even look directly at the boss but off in a corner somewhere.

Many bosses can easily detect from the way a person talks and acts whether that person lacks confidence. A faltering voice and defensive physical posture are more revealing than the words being spoken and provide the boss with a definite negotiating edge.

Because we fear losing the job, we enter into the negotiation in a mentally defensive posture. This posture automatically gives the boss offensive negotiating power. No wonder many of us fail.

Fear of loss is relative. The greater the fear, the less the likelihood of success. For example, the longer a person has been with the company and the more benefits that person has accrued, such as pension and insurance, the greater will be the fear of loss of employment because there seems to be so much more to lose.

It is therefore highly important to eliminate fear of loss of employment prior to asking your boss for a raise. You should do this in any manner that will work for you since different people are influenced by different situations and events. You can even go so far as to line up new employment to fall back on in the event your raise request is refused. In fact, having another comparable posi-tion lined up at the time you ask for a raise can be an excellent method of increasing your nego-tiating leverage and thus enhancing your chances of success. If you can point out during the discussion that you are in demand and have another job offer, your boss may be the one to experience fear of loss—fear of losing you. In such a case your boss would be the one negotiating from a negative, defensive position with the offense switching to you. That is ideal for you and a position that will materially increase your likelihood of success.

Fear of Failure

The second major reason for failure is, ironically, fear of failure itself. We fear that our request for a raise will be rejected. We therefore have placed ourselves in the same defensive position as when we experience fear of losing our job. In fact, often when we seek a raise we experience both fears and thus put ourselves in double jeopardy.

Remedying fear of failure can be accomplished by developing a positive state of mind prior to conferring with the boss about the raise. Certainly, having other comparable employment lined up prior to conferring with the boss will alleviate fear. The ability to waltz right out the door in the event of rejection and go to work elsewhere is a great confidence booster. But in addition to having new employment lined up there is another important way to eliminate fear and that is to consciously push fear of failure out of your thoughts. Replace the fear with positive thinking.

Use mental practice to your advantage. Visualize yourself as succeeding, see yourself as actually talking with your boss. Form a mental picture of the scene and visualize the boss agreeing with your position. See your boss nodding yes to your request for a raise. Fear of failure cannot exist in such a positive mental environment.

Rehearse your approach to your boss just as an actress rehearses her lines for her role. Imagine the actual dialogue between you and your boss. This rehearsal should include actually asking your boss as if your boss were present. Since your request is so important to your ultimate success, mentally rehearse to such an extent that even your tone of voice can be developed to reflect your poise and confidence.

While you rehearse, mentally place yourself in the role of your boss and raise objections to your request. This self-imposed cross-examination allows you to anticipate any objections and to practice dealing with the objections calmly and efficiently.

For example, one possible objection the boss might raise is that a similar raise would have to be given to other employees who work in the same or in a similar capacity as you do. Depending upon the circumstances of your job, you might counter that the objection is not justified since your job is fairly unique within the company or, your performance far exceeds that of others in the same or a similar capacity. If you have mentally raised and dealt with as many potential objections as you realistically can think of prior to the time you actually confer with your boss, your confidence will be greater and so will your chances of success.

THE NEXT STEP: SELECT THE BEST TIME AND PLACE

As we have previously advised, select the time and place that best enhance your negotiating posture. The Bible teaches that there is a time for "every purpose under the heaven" including a time to "keep silence, and a time to speak."[1] Pick a time when you are at your best as well as a time when your boss will be in the most receptive mood. You can determine this largely from your own experience and observations. Is your boss usually irritable on Monday? Is Friday his or her best day? Plot your timing so that you avoid any predictable bad moods.

A common and costly error is to go into the boss's office to ask for the salary increase. The boss's office is his or her home field, which gives the boss a decided edge. You should therefore seek your salary increase either on your home field or at a neutral location, perhaps in the lunchroom, hallway, or even in an elevator or restaurant. Even a chance meeting at any of these places may provide you with the opportunity to confront the boss.

In your place of work, whether your office or anywhere else you perform your daily tasks, you have the edge. It is there that you are most comfortable and familiar with the surroundings and environment. It is there that your boss will be the most awkward. You will feel comfortable and your boss, uncomfortable. That is the reason why it is not unusual when a boss is confronted in your

---

1. Ecclesiastes 3:1–8.

environment or in a neutral environment to say, "Let's discuss this in my office" or, "Let's go to my office and talk it over." The boss wants to go to a comfortable and familiar setting, one that gives the boss the edge. Some bosses do this automatically, not really knowing why but knowing that they feel uncomfortable in your environment or in a neutral setting.

You should be prepared for the possibility that your boss will suggest that you both retreat to your boss's office to discuss the matter. You might counter by relating that there is some pressing reason why you must remain where you both are, such as you must perform a task that is necessary to the company. The reason, of course, must be genuine and suitable to force the boss to remain where you both are and deal with your request for a raise. If you cannot come up with a genuine reason, you may be forced to discuss the matter in your boss's office as your boss has requested. If that is the case, don't allow this sudden switch to environments to affect your confidence and ruin your planned approach. If you detect that happening, relate to your boss that you would prefer to discuss the matter at a later time. That way you will have sufficient time to compose yourself and reexamine your approach in light of having to discuss the matter in your boss's office.

If you discuss the matter in your boss's office, try to have your boss sitting and you standing, looking down at your boss. The reason is that your height will provide you with a psychological edge. There is an old movie where two characters are playing the part of competing dictators. Both are sitting in barber chairs getting a shave. The chairs are the kind that can be elevated by pushing a lever. When one pushes the lever to elevate his chair higher than the other so that he can look down on the other and thus assume the dominant position, the other responded in kind so that they both keep rising until they hit the ceiling. It was a comedy, of course, but the psychological principle was accurate. The one that was the highest was in the dominant position—the position you want to be in when discussing a salary increase in your boss's office. So stand in front of your boss's desk with your boss seated behind the desk to deprive your boss of some of the home field advantage.

THE NEED TO INCREASE YOUR NEGOTIATING LEVERAGE

Once you have diminished your fear of loss and failure and have settled on the proper time and place, the next step is to increase your leverage. Leverage is the process of increasing negotiating power to attain the desired result.

One good way to increase your leverage is to seek your raise soon after you have done something special on your job. Perhaps, for example, you closed an important deal that will benefit both your boss and the company. Perhaps you assisted in ironing out a complicated problem that had been worrying your boss.

If you can approach your boss soon after you have done something special that will either directly or indirectly benefit the boss and the organization, you will have significantly increased your negotiating leverage. Your boss will probably find it extremely difficult to turn down your request for a raise just after you have performed an outstanding service.

Don't try to improve your leverage by comparing yourself to others. "I'm worth more than so and so" is poor form. Negotiate on the basis of *your* productivity and accomplishments.

THE POWER OF YOUR APPEARANCE AND SPOKEN WORDS

To add to what we have already said about the nonverbal communication factors of appearance and voice, be certain when you ask for that raise that your personal appearance is neat and attractive and does not detract from what you are saying. Dressing and looking as if you are poor and need the money may work in other circumstances, but not when asking for a raise. If that approach strikes your boss as phoney, it could work to your detriment.

When you speak, do so clearly and get right to the point. Most bosses appreciate frankness and resent employees who use the guise of talking about other business and then tack on a request for a raise at the end. That resentment can lead to rejection.

This is not to say, however, that you should ask for a raise immediately. On the contrary, getting your boss in an affirmative frame of mind should be your preliminary objective. It can be done easily by referring to something you know will be agreeable—the nice weather, a win by a local sports team, or a community charity drive.

You say to your boss, "I see the charity drive met its goal." Your boss may reply, "Yes."

You then say, "It is really great the way people respond to help those that are less fortunate."

Again your boss may reply, "Yes, it is."

That is all you need. Your boss is in the right, positive frame of mind and has said yes twice. You can then state the purpose of your visit, namely that you deserve and want a raise.

ANSWER THE KEY QUESTION—WHY?

Too often, a person seeking a raise takes for granted that the boss is fully aware of the reasons why a raise should be given. The trouble with that approach is that it fails to acknowledge that bosses are human and, under the pressure of their job and the passage of time, they tend to take one day at a time without remembering the past. As a consequence, it is important when asking for a raise to fully explain the reasons why you should be given that raise. Your explanation can be condensed into a few well-chosen sentences, but make the information complete enough to jog the boss's memory. Never take for granted that the boss has all this knowledge readily available.

Numerous raise requests fail because the employee doesn't realize that the boss may not be completely aware of all the circumstances or the reasons behind the request. The result is that the request is denied and the employee departs in an angry state of mind, feeling that the boss does not fully appreciate the employee's fine efforts on behalf of the company.

SHOULD YOU ASK FOR A DEFINITE AMOUNT?

It is best not to ask for a specific amount. A better approach is to allow your boss to set the initial amount. The reason is that your boss may give you a higher increase than you may ask for; whereas, if you initially ask for a definite amount, you may have set the upper limit of what you will get.

For example, if you ask your boss for a hundred-dollar-a-week raise, you have probably set the upper limit. If, on the other hand, you demonstrate why you deserve a raise and then ask for it, your boss may give you more than one hundred dollars a week. Even if your boss insists that you name a figure, you can counter by saying that you want a reasonable amount, commensurate with the good work you have been doing.

Again the burden of setting the raise figure is shifted to the boss, and, as related, the boss may give you a larger raise than you anticipated. If your boss again refuses to name a figure and asks you for one, you can then relate the amount of the raise that you think is reasonable and realistic. You have thus not lost anything. What's more, if your boss declines twice and gets you to set your own raise figure, it indicates you have a highly capable and intelligent boss who realizes that it is more desirable to have you set the amount of the raise.

NEGOTIATING A HIGHER SALARY
WHEN APPLYING FOR A NEW JOB

In the past, women have trusted employers to pay them the highest available salary. Today's woman is learning that the employment interview is an important place to negotiate salary because a lower starting salary can mean a serious loss of income for years to come.

Before your interview, you should, of course, do your homework and know the true market value of the position for which you are applying. Having this knowledge, acquired from such sources as colleagues, employment agencies, and want ads, gives you confidence. You also should have in mind a salary range from a high hoped-for figure to your minimum acceptable amount.

Don't start off with a discussion of salary. Ask about the company and the details of the job first. Let the prospective employer bring up the subject of money. Just as in the situation of asking for a raise, it is wise to get the employer to name a figure or a range to protect you from naming too low an amount.

Emphasize your accomplishments, *not* your needs. Show how your past accomplishments relate to the position you are applying for. Keep your negotiating flexible and be alert to all the options that may be available to you.

CHAPTER 9

Negotiating a Loan

Virtually every woman who assumes a degree of family responsibility or takes her place in the business world will need to borrow money for either personal or business use. Whether or not a favorable loan is obtained will, to a large degree, depend upon the woman's ability to negotiate.

Although loans can be for short durations, such as 30 to 60 days, many loans are long-term commitments of five years or longer. Real estate loans can run as long as 30 years or more. Borrowing money is therefore an important commitment that requires careful thought and preparation. Once the loan papers have been signed, second thoughts about either the propriety of the loan or whether the loan cost was low enough are no longer viable unless the loan can be refinanced.

BE FULLY AWARE OF THE LENDER'S MOTIVES FOR MAKING THE LOAN

Lenders make loans for basically one reason: *to make a profit*. They are therefore going to attempt to make the loan at the highest true interest rate possible in order to maximize their income from that loan.

Never lose sight of this fact when you prepare for and approach a lender. Avoid falling into the pitfall of thinking that the lender is a nice person who is willing to make the loan in order to look out for your welfare. Don't allow the lender's commercials about those "wonderful people who are anxious to help you" to lull you into thinking you won't need to skilfully negotiate in order to attain a favorable loan. Consider the commercials for what they are—paid ads designed to influence you to do business with one lender instead of the lender's competition.

A second major objective that the lender is trying to accomplish when making you a loan is to get as much security for the loan as possible in order to eliminate to the greatest degree possible any potential loss in the event the loan is not paid off. Here again, don't be influenced by any nice person image the lender is trying to portray. If the lender wants you to put up real estate or stocks and bonds as security for the loan, the lender's purpose is solely to be able to use your property to satisfy the loan in the event you default.

PERSONAL GUARANTEES

Frequently, lenders seek personal guarantees on loans as additional security. On a personal loan you, or course, will already be personally liable. But if you are seeking the loan on behalf of a corporation that is a separate legal entity, the lender may well ask that you personally guarantee to pay the loan in the event the corporation fails to pay. If at all possible, refuse. If the lender persists and will not make the loan without your personal guarantee and you cannot find another lender who will make the loan without your personal guarantee, then you should be fully aware of what you are guaranteeing.

For example, take the case of two individuals who started a new business venture. They formed a corporation and obtained a loan with both people guaranteeing the loan in the event the corporation defaulted. Later, one of the individuals terminated all relationship with the company but the lender continued to make loans to the corporation. Later when the corporation defaulted, the lender sued both individuals for the amount of the outstanding loans because both had signed a "continuing guarantee," which meant that both guaranteed all loans to the corporation irrespective of when the loans were made.

The moral is that if you cannot obtain the money without personally guaranteeing repayment and still deem it wise to go ahead with the loan, be certain that you guarantee only the immediate loan and only on a conditional basis, which means that the lender must first seek payment from the principal borrower before proceeding against you. This condition prevents the lender from making future loans that you will be required to guarantee. In addition, it prevents the lender from getting lazy and automatically seeking payment from you in the event there is a default without first attempting to get the money from the principal borrower.

ALWAYS DETERMINE THE TRUE INTEREST RATE

Your basic negotiating objective is to obtain the loan at the lowest possible cost. This not only means the lowest possible interest rate but also means terms and conditions that do not increase the true interest rate over the stated or advertised interest rate.

Frequently, loans are made on terms and conditions that, in substance, increase the stated interest rate. For example, the loan terms may provide that in the event the borrower pays off the loan prior to the due date, a prepayment penalty will be charged. Thus, if the borrower decides to pay the loan ahead of the regular due date, the lender will assess an additional fee that increases the actual cost of the loan.

Now you may take the position that if the stated interest rate is acceptable at the time the loan is made, the borrower would not be inclined to prepay the loan and, hence, with no prepayment, no penalty. The problem with that approach is that it violates one of the most important rules of successful negotiation—*always work to keep your options open.*

Since no one can predict the future with any certainty, who knows what opportunities might arise? It is both a desirable and a sound practice to see to it that you are in a position to take advantage of each opportunity.

For example, let's assume you obtain a loan at 11 percent interest with an additional penalty of one percent of the outstanding loan balance if the loan is paid off prior to its due date. What if soon after the loan if finalized, you discover a new lender who will make the same loan for only 8 percent? In order to take advantage of that 8 percent rate, you will have to pay the prepayment penalty on the 11 percent loan. Payment of the penalty, of course, increases the 11 percent rate whereas, if the 11 percent loan had been negotiated without any prepayment penalty, you would have the option of acquiring the same money at only 8 percent and paying off the 11 percent loan with money borrowed at 8 percent. This amounts to a 3 percent reduction (less any loan closing expenses) in the loan cost.

As an additional illustration, sometimes prepayment of a loan is not allowed for a specific period. Perhaps the loan is for ten years with no prepayment right until after the third year. Here again, the result of such a restrictive prepayment provision is to prevent you from refinancing within that three-year period and thus to potentially increase the cost of the loan.

Another common practice is to require the borrower to keep a minimum balance on deposit with the lender, usually about 10 percent of the loan. This restriction also adds to the loan cost because the lender has use of the minimum funds either at no cost or at a much lower cost, and the lender can lend out those funds to another borrower. If, for example, you borrow $10,000 at a stated interest rate of 9 percent for one year and the lender requires that you maintain a minimum balance of $1,000, you are really paying more for the loan because you are getting use of only $9,000. Even though the stated interest rate is 9 percent, the true interest rate is really 10 percent. Nine percent interest on $10,000 for one year is $900. Dividing that $900 by $9,000, which is the net amount of the loan you are actually able to use, you come out with 10 percent as the true loan cost.

Whenever a loan is being negotiated, consider *all* of the terms to be certain that provisions that can or do result in a greater true loan cost over the stated loan cost are fully considered. Either eliminate or vary these provisions or agree upon them only after you are certain you understand all the ramifications and are willing to live with them.

OBTAIN ANY AVAILABLE ADVANCE INFORMATION

Try to get as much advance information about the lending practices of at least three lenders prior to actually negotiating the terms of the loan. Most banks and savings and loans have standard printed loan forms that they will make available. With this information, you will be able to carefully examine and compare the various provisions of each lender before deciding which one to approach first. You will no doubt find that the provisions in the documents are heavily slanted in favor of the lender and you will need to know this information in order to better prepare your negotiating strategy.

A word of caution, however. We are recommending that you acquire the loan forms for study and comparison, not to fill in. Make only one loan application after you have done your comparison shopping. Why? Because the fact that you have applied (whether or not you get the money) goes in your credit file.

SHOP FOR LENDERS AS YOU DO FOR OTHER PURCHASES

Lenders compete for business like other merchants. The only difference is that the lender's product is money. Shop around and don't forget to let every potential lender know that you are shopping in order to create fear of the loss of your business and increase your negotiating leverage.

HAVE A DEFINITE LOAN COST OBJECTIVE

Whenever you approach a lender, it is important to have a definite loan cost objective in mind. For example, assume after due deliberation you set as your objective getting a loan at a true loan cost of no higher than 9 percent. This decision tends to put more pressure on you both during preparation and actual negotiation. You will be forced to work harder and do a better job. Your senses will be more acute as you set out to accomplish your objective.

This method is far better than merely trying to obtain a vague objective such as "the best or lowest true loan cost possible," as many borrowers do.

TAKE ADVANTAGE OF NEGOTIATING LEVERAGE

Don't forget the concept of leverage discussed earlier. In order to gain the most favorable loan terms, one form of leverage is to seek ways to take advantage of the lender's fear of losing your business. If, for example, you are negotiating a personal loan from a bank, it is better to go to a smaller bank, preferably where you and perhaps others in your family or in your business have accounts. Letting the banker know at some appropriate time that you and your family or associates, collectively, are good bank customers, tends to create an environment that facilitates a favorable loan because the lender may be fearful of losing a lot of business. If you attempted the same technique with a large bank, little fear of loss would exist since smaller accounts may represent only a minor part of the large bank's overall business. Threatened loss would, therefore, have a negligible impact upon the large bank.

The safest rule to follow is to look for lenders where your financial muscle will create the greatest fear of loss of your business.

To further illustrate, one of John's clients wanted to negotiate a business loan from a bank. The client was a substantial bank customer, not only with checking and savings accounts but also with many employees who also had accounts there. Initially, the bank was willing to make the loan at 2 percent above the prime interest rate. (The prime rate is *supposed* to be the rate that banks lend money to their blue chip, or most solid customers, the theory being that the customers of lesser stability will be charged more because the bank takes more risk with them. Actually, the prime rate is a fallacy that lenders hide behind and use as a tool to lend money at high interest rates. Many customers with plenty of financial leverage with the lender consistently obtain loans for less than the prime rate. Thus, don't be fooled when the banker attempts to justify charging you a higher interest rate by relating what the prime lending rate is and that you will have to pay more than the prime rate).

After it was clearly pointed out to the bank what an important customer John's client was, the bank, due mainly to fear of loss of the client's business, made the loan for 2 percent *below* the prime rate or a reduction of 4 percent over the initially asked for interest rate.

If you do not as yet command sufficient clout to use fear of loss of your business as leverage, you might consider stressing your anticipated growth. Emphasize that if the lender is inclined to give you favorable loan terms now, the institution can have greater assurance of your continued business. Strive to increase your negotiating leverage in any legitimate way possible.

DON'T WAIT UNTIL THE LAST MINUTE

You should avoid waiting until there is a pressing need for money before seeking a loan. This waiting puts unnecessary pressure on you so that when you try to negotiate with the lender your need for money is so urgent that you are unable to concentrate. What's more, you are less able to negotiate boldly with that if-I-can't-get-the-loan-terms-that-suit-me-I'll-go-elsewhere attitude that is so necessary to your negotiating self-confidence.

Remember, too, that many lenders are experienced in both negotiating loans and dealing with people. If they discover from your attitude, or what you are telling them, or from the financial information you present that your need for the money is urgent, that knowledge will increase the lender's leverage. Lenders use that kind of knowledge to get better terms for themselves, such as higher interest rates, greater security in the form of personal guarantees, or a pledge of other assets.

Whenever possible, apply for the loan before the need for the money becomes acute. This will relieve you of unnecessary negotiating pressure and decrease the lender's leverage. In addition, it will allow you to concentrate fully on negotiating as well as to shop around with various lenders in order to negotiate the best loan possible.

AVOID UNFAVORABLE PRECEDENT SETTING

Unfavorable precedents can be particularly costly when negotiating for loans. As an example, John agreed to represent a client who, prior to John's representation, was having to give full security for each loan even though the client's net worth was substantially in excess of the amount of the loan. Upon checking, John found that the client had originally borrowed money many years ago with full security and the bank was automatically continuing the practice every time a new loan was taken out. The earlier precedent had become a routine process.

Be aware of the danger of unfavorable precedent setting and try to eliminate any burdensome loan requirements that the lender is attempting to impose upon you. If you cannot avoid the requirement and are unable to get the loan elsewhere, attempt to restrict any requirements to the present loan.

For example, assume the lender requires a personal guarantee by you for a loan made to a company that you operate or work for. You might specify *at the time the loan is negotiated* that in the event the loan is paid in full on the due date that meeting this condition is sufficient to establish your credit so that any future loans will not require any personal guarantee. At first blush this might sound like an unrealistic condition imposed on your part but it really isn't if you exert enough negotiating leverage on the lender. Remember most lenders want the business and will, if they must, make numerous concessions to get the business, especially if the lender feels you are potentially a solid, reliable customer. Unfortunately, many borrowers fail to exert themselves or ask for concessions.

PRESENT GOOD NEGOTIATING FORM

Remember that as with other kinds of negotiating, how you present yourself, the way you look, talk, and act, play an important role in the negotiating process. Also, any written material that you present to the lender, such as profit and loss statements and balance sheets, should be prepared to make a favorable impression.

Since one of the lender's objectives is to be certain that the loan will be repaid, the lender's confidence in you and your credibility will serve as your negotiating ally and increase your power. This confidence can largely be generated by your appearance and behavior.

As we have already seen, your tone of voice is part of your negotiating form. Speak confidently and don't allow the lender's questions to put you on the defensive. For example, if you are seeking a loan and the lender says, "Do you mean that you want $20,000? Money is really tight and the prime interest rate is 15 percent," the lender is trying to put you on the defensive and set you up to pay a substantially higher loan cost than the prime interest rate.

If you cave in at this point it will probably be reflected in your voice. Hang on and make your voice firm and say something like, "I'm a good customer of this bank and money should be available for me. If the terms aren't suitable I guess I'll have to go elsewhere. I'm planning to check with other lenders anyway."

This type of reply should allow you to maintain the offensive. You have called the lender's attention to the fact that you are a good customer. You have tactfully slipped in—without threatening—that you might take your business elsewhere, and so your answer is power packed, placing you in a good negotiating posture with the lender.

CHAPTER 10

Negotiating Leases and Subleases

Renting property normally calls for a written agreement between the property owner and the renter, which is called a *lease*. Written leases are common when you are renting property for business use or apartment and home rentals, particularly rentals that go beyond a month in duration. The lease sets forth the terms and conditions of the rental agreement between the property owner and the renter. From a negotiating standpoint, both the property owner and the renter should strive to have those terms and conditions that each considers beneficial included in the written lease.

A *sublease* is an agreement, again usually in writing, between the party leasing the property and a new party. The person leasing the property from the property owner is called the *lessee* in her or his relationship with the property owner, and the *sublessor* in her or his relationship with the new party, who is called the *sublessee*.

Terms of the sublease usually vary from the terms of the original lease, which is called the *prime lease*. For example, the prime lease might be for a period of five years with an annual rental of $20,000. The lessee might then sublease the property to the sublessee for a period of four years with an annual rental of $22,000.

Legally, no privity of contract exists between the property owner and the sublessee. What this means is that the property owner must deal only with the lessee and only the lessee can deal with the sublessee.

To illustrate, let's go back to our previous example in which the property owner leases the property to the lessee for a five-year term with an annual rental of $20,000; the lessee then subleases the property to the sublessee for a four-year term with an annual rental of $22,000. If the sublessee in this case fails to pay the $22,000 rent to the lessee and the lessee, as a consequence, fails to pay the $20,000 rent to the property owner, the property owner cannot go after the sublessee, but must seek a remedy against the lessee. Only the lessee can seek a remedy against the sublessee.

This distinction can play an important role in negotiating a sublease for two essential reasons. First, since the terms and conditions of the sublease differ from those of the prime lease, you, the negotiator, should seek an opportunity to examine the prime lease in order to determine how the terms of the prime lease differ. This knowledge will greatly strengthen your bargaining position. If, for example, the lessee was able to negotiate favorable lease terms from the property owner, you can learn what they are by examining the prime lease and you can try to get the same favorable terms from the lessee in your sublease.

Secondly, it is important for you to be certain that the prime lease gives the lessee authority to sublease the property on the terms and conditions you negotiated in order to insure that you will have undisturbed possession and use of the property. What's more, the sublease should include a provision that the lessee has full authority to sublease the property on the terms and conditions of the sublease. If it turns out that the lessee has no such authority, you, the sublessee, can seek a remedy against the lessee for violation of such a provision. But seeking a remedy can be both costly and time consuming and can also cancel any favorable sublease provisions that you were able to negotiate with the lessee. Consequently, it is normally better for you to examine the prime lease to be certain that the prime lease gives the lessee full authority to sublease the property on your terms and conditions.

The relationship between the property owner, the lessee-sublessor, and the sublessee is further clarified in Table 10.1. Figure A represents the property owner; Figure B represents the lessee-sublessor; and Figure C represents the sublessee.

If you are the *property owner* or are representing the property owner, you can see the importance of including a provision in the prime lease that either prohibits subleasing or allows it only after the property owner has given written approval. Such a provision allows the property owner

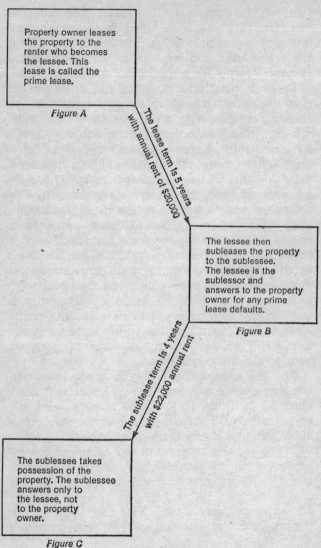

Property owner leases the property to the renter who becomes the lessee. This lease is called the prime lease.

Figure A

The lease term is 5 years with annual rent of $20,000

The lessee then subleases the property to the sublessee. The lessee is the sublessor and answers to the property owner for any prime lease defaults.

Figure B

The sublease term is 4 years with $22,000 annual rent

The sublessee takes possession of the property. The sublessee answers only to the lessee, not to the property owner.

Figure C

Table 10.1

to carefully determine whether the sublessee is financially capable of paying the sublease rent to the lessee and also whether the sublessee is the type of tenant that will maintain the property in good condition. Otherwise, if the sublessee fails to pay the rent or lets the property run down and the lessee, as a consequence, fails to pay rent to the property owner or does nothing to stop the sublessee from letting the property deteriorate, it may force the property owner to proceed legally against the lessee, which, as previously related, can be both costly and time consuming.

If you are the lessee or are representing the lessee, you can see the importance of negotiating a prime lease provision that allows the lessee to sublease the property on an unrestricted basis. Such a provision would allow the lessee to sublease the property for a higher rent than the rent the lessee is required to pay under the prime lease and thus make a profit. In addition, such a provision can also provide the lessee with excellent business flexibility. For example, assume the lessee opens a business on the leased property but later circumstances, such as ill health, make running the business difficult. If the prime lease allows the lessee complete right to sublease, the lessee can sublease the property to another party who wants to run the business and the sublease can be for a larger amount than the lessee is required to pay to the property owner. The lessee has thus not only obtained relief from running the business but managed to earn a profit as well.

LEASE ASSIGNMENTS

An assignment of a lease differs from a sublease in that when the lessee assigns the lease to another party (called the *assignee*), the lessee parts with his or her whole interest in the lease so that the assignee, in essence, steps into the shoes of and becomes the lessee on the same lease terms and conditions as the lessee. The lessee, however, remains fully liable to the property owner in the event the assignee defaults under the lease and the property owner can take legal action against the lessee *or* the assignee.

From a negotiating standpoint, the same considerations that apply to the sublease apply to a lease assignment for the property owner, the lessee, and the assignee. The only basic difference is that the lessee normally assigns the whole lease and therefore does not take any profit by charging the assignee a higher rent than the lessee was required to pay under the lease.

Table 10.2 further simplifies the relationship among the property owner, the lessee-assignor, and the assignee. Figure A represents the property owner; Figure B represents the lessee-assignor; and Figure C represents the assignee.

THE TIME WHEN YOUR NEGOTIATING LEVERAGE IS GREATEST

Recently, when a large shopping center refused to renew the leases of ten stores in the center, many of the store owners and managers were naturally bitter. One woman manager said, "They [the shopping center management] just said, 'Out

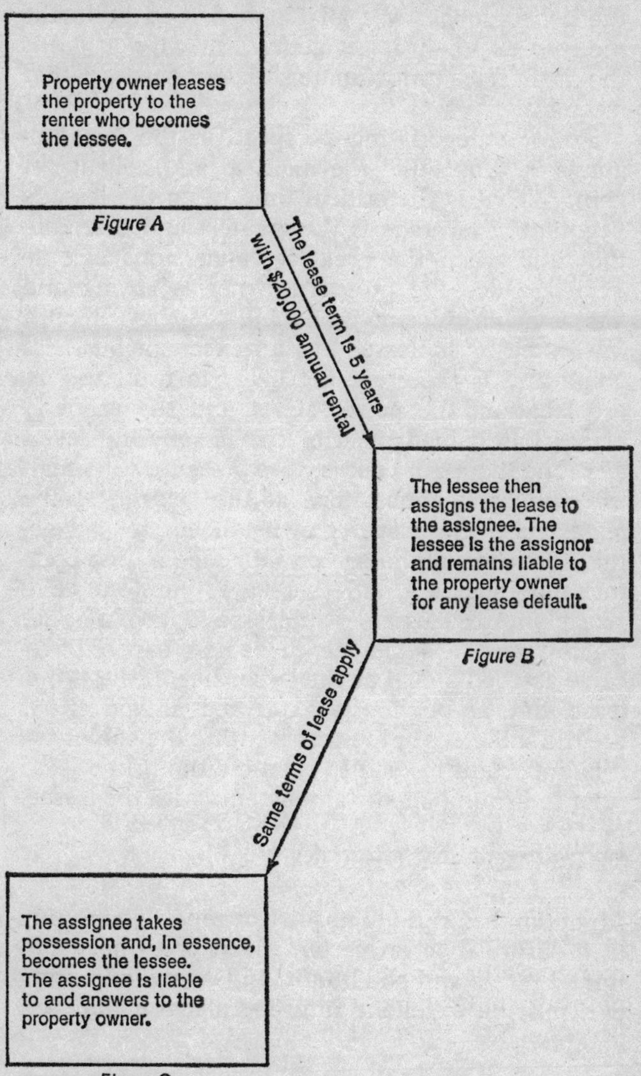

Property owner leases the property to the renter who becomes the lessee.

Figure A

The lease term is 5 years with $20,000 annual rental

The lessee then assigns the lease to the assignee. The lessee is the assignor and remains liable to the property owner for any lease default.

Figure B

Same terms of lease apply

The assignee takes possession and, in essence, becomes the lessee. The assignee is liable to and answers to the property owner.

Figure C

Table 10.2

the door you go.' We all felt bad. You build the mall up and help it get going. And all you get is the door." This unfortunate situation occurs rather frequently.

From a negotiating perspective, the key language is "You build the mall up and help it get going." That is the critical time when the lessee's negotiating leverage is the greatest and therefore the time when the greatest concessions can be gained. Once the property owner is strong and has a viable, income-producing property or once the lessee or sublessee has an excellent business going and is therefore not likely to want to lose the location, the power shifts and the property owner has gained most of the negotiating leverage. The moral, of course, is to press for the greatest gains and concessions at the signing of the lease when the property owner needs to "get going," or when the lessee or sublessee is just commencing business and there are therefore valid reasons for the lessee or sublessee to have a better leasing deal. A sublessee, of course, can only receive as good a deal as the lessee has in the prime lease and, as previously explained, if you either are the sublessee or are representing the sublessee, it is important for you to examine the prime lease prior to firming up any agreements with the lessee.

THE MAGIC OF OPTIONS

An option is a right to acquire or renew something at a future date on certain fixed or to be determined terms and conditions. In leasing, an option can provide excellent future protection and can avert situations such as what happened to the tenants at the shopping center.

For example, suppose you want to start a new business and you don't want to commit yourself to a long lease because you aren't sure if the business will be successful. On the other hand, if the business is successful, you don't want to be evicted when your lease expires. The solution is simple— take advantage of the *option*. Lease the premises for a short period, say one or two years, which obligates you or your company for only that period. Include in the lease an option to renew, preferably on the same terms and conditions as the original lease. The option renewal can be for any additional number or years or successive number of years that you deem desirable. For instance, the option might provide that you or your business can renew the lease for two more years after the original lease has elapsed and, after the two-year-option renewal time has passed, you or your business have the right to renew for two more years or longer, as you deem necessary, as long as the exact number of years is specified in the lease. This provision allows you to analyze your business after each period to determine whether you want to continue it. That is one of the advantages of the option: Only you have the right to renew. The property owner can neither force you to renew nor terminate your option. You have thus monopolized virtually all of the negotiating leverage for any lease renewals simply by use of the option.

Take another example. Assume you want to lease an apartment but only want to commit yourself for a short time because you may soon be moving out of the area. The property owner, however, wants you to sign a lease for at least one year. You propose a six-month lease with an option to renew for six additional months in the event you do not leave the area. Landlords will often agree, especially when there are several vacancies. The lease merely states that your option will be exercised if you do not leave the area. The option has thus provided you with excellent freedom to move about without the burden of being obligated to a longer term lease.

THE BEST TIME TO OBTAIN FAVORABLE OPTIONS

The shopping center incident clearly shows that the best time to obtain options is at the outset when the property owner needs you as a tenant to occupy the space. Once the property owner can afford to shop for and choose tenants, most of the negotiating leverage is with the owner, thus making it highly unlikely that any favorable options can be obtained. Push hard for favorable options during the negotiations on the initial lease or sublease—the time when your leverage is greatest and you have the best chance of getting favorable renewal options.

OPTIONS CAN ALSO BE USEFUL FOR PURCHASES

Whenever leasing business or personal property, consider whether you would like to purchase the property at a future date. An excellent method to insure that you have the right to purchase is to negotiate an option to purchase into the lease. You can frequently get such a purchase option on favorable terms because property owners are so eager to lease that, through fear of losing you as a potential tenant, they will give you the right to purchase the property.

If you do get an option to purchase, it is best to negotiate the terms and conditions then and have them inserted in the lease rather than at the time you want to exercise the option. The reason is that if your business becomes highly successful, the property owner will undoubtedly want more for the property than when your business first started. Moreover, inflation means that the property is bound to be worth more at the later date if the property is properly maintained and located in a viable area.

WHO SHOULD PREPARE THE LEASE OR SUBLEASE?

Whenever possible, have your attorney prepare the lease or sublease. This allows you to insert those provisions that are beneficial to your interests. Experience has shown that many of those beneficial provisions will go unchallenged during the negotiation and most of the lease or sublease will remain precisely as your lawyer drafted it. Any preparation costs are therefore more than offset by those favorable terms that were accepted.

For instance, let's say you are the lessee and have a lease drafted with an initial term of three years. You also include an option provision allowing you to renew the lease on the same terms and conditions as the initial term for five additional years after the initial term has expired and for two successive five-year terms thereafter. The property owner doesn't contest giving you the option but proposes a three-year renewal term at a 10 percent rental increase at the time each of the options is exercised. The result is that the options remain in the lease except that they are for three years instead of five and for a 10 percent increase instead of on the same terms and conditions as the initial three-year term.

You are now in an excellent position in the event the business turns out to be profitable. In addition, before you decide whether to exercise any of the options, you can compare the rental increase of 10 percent to the cost of leasing similar property and either exercise each option or rent less expensive property. You can take into consideration that a 10 percent rental increase amounts to only a three and one-third percent increase per year, over each three-year lease period. This will undoubtedly be far less than the annual rate of inflation. This approach gives you excellent flexibility in your occupancy of the property.

WHAT TO DO WHEN CONFRONTED WITH A WRITTEN LEASE

Property owners usually have leases or subleases typed or printed in fancy form that can appear formidable. You can be sure that in most instances the provisions of these documents will be heavily slanted in favor of the property owner.

Don't allow these formal documents to force you into a defensive negotiating posture. Rather, treat them for what they really are—merely pieces of paper containing the property owner's proposals for renting the property to you.

Once you have received the written lease or sublease from the property owner (or sublessor), ask for time to examine it and take as much time as you feel you need. Read each provision carefully and get legal advice if you need clarification of any of the terms.

For example, if you are leasing property for business use, the chances are good that the owner will try to have the rent based on a percentage of gross sales of the business over and above the fixed rent. You should completely understand what gross sales means, as well as the financial consequences of such a lease provision. You might, for instance, be asked to pay an annual rent of $18,000 with an additional rent of 6 percent on annual gross sales in excess of $300,000. Thus, if sales for the first year of business were $400,000, the proposed rental would amount to $24,000 ($18,000 fixed rent plus 6 percent of the $100,000 difference between the actual sales of $400,000 and the $300,000 base sales figure in the lease).

If you understand every provision in the lease, you will be able to choose which provisions to accept and which to reject or alter. Obviously, the greater the term of the lease and the greater the amount of rental you or your business is required to pay, the more intense effort you should put into understanding all aspects of the lease. Don't wait until problems occur to understand all the fine print in the lease.

You *do not* have to be a legal expert to understand what the submitted lease or sublease provisions mean because you can always get a clarification from a knowledgeable source. But you *do* have to understand them in order to negotiate effectively.

MAKE CONCESSIONS ON NONFINANCIAL ASPECTS

Obviously, in many lease negotiations, circumstances will occur that require you to make concessions. Give-and-take occurs, frequently when the parties have reached an impasse on a particular issue. If you must make concessions, always try to make them on nonfinancial issues.

For example, assume you are negotiating a lease and the property owner wants you to pay for all outside maintenance of the property. You, on another issue, want the property owner to give you thirty days notice in writing of any defaults of your lease, and you want the opportunity to correct any such defaults within sixty days. You might concede by reducing the thirty days to twenty and the sixty days to fifty if the property owner will drop the demand that you pay for outside maintenance. Your concessions are nonfinancial and pertain to the mechanics of the lease in the event of a default.

MAKE CONCESSIONS THAT REDUCE YOUR FINANCIAL COMMITMENT

If you are unable to get the property owner to make nonfinancial concessions, the next approach is to attempt to get the owner to agree to concessions that reduce or limit your financial commitment. On long-term leases, even small financial concessions can result in large savings.

An example would be if you are negotiating a business lease and the property owner will not budge on requiring you to pay for insurance that covers fire and other hazards. You want the lease so you agree to pay for the insurance. Before you agree, however, get the owner to settle on a maximum property value for which you will be required to insure. As the property appreciates, as most property that is well located and maintained does, your cash outlay for insurance premiums will not also automatically increase unless, of course, the insurance company increases rates.

Another example of setting an upper limit on your potential future expenses is with shopping center property. Many shopping centers require their tenants to share the cost of utilities and maintenance of the common areas such as hallways and parking lots. If the shopping center is well established, with tenants waiting in line to get space, new tenants will possess little negotiating leverage and might not be able to negotiate a ceiling on potential future expenses. If, however, the center is new or is struggling and needs tenants, or the business you intend to operate is either strong or unique and will give the owner a better mix of stores, chances are good that you will be able to negotiate such a ceiling on future expenses for the common areas.

LOOK FOR OPPORTUNITIES TO EMPHASIZE YOUR NEED FOR FLEXIBILITY

If you intend to lease the property for business purposes, always look for opportunities during the negotiating to emphasize your need for flexibility in the lease terms in order to make your business successful. A successful business, of course, means that there will be greater stability for the property owner and thus greater insurance that the owner will receive rents over the life of the lease. Emphasizing this need for flexibility and that it will ultimately pay off for the owner as well as for you, is an excellent technique. Use it to try to get favorable lease provisions, such as options, the right to assign or sublease without written approval from the property owner, and ceilings on potential future expenses.

CHAPTER **11**

Negotiating as
a Consumer

Hardly a day goes by that we don't buy a product
or a service as consumers. What stands out in our
minds is the time we got that lemon or a dud and
had to fight to get a replacement or a refund.

When we occasionally run into uncaring bu-
reaucracy, we may be tempted to let it go after a
half-hearted attempt to get redress. Many times
we just reason that, "It's too much trouble." This
may be smart reasoning if the item sells for $2.98,
but if the cost is greater, in the hundreds or more,
it behooves us to seek either a new item or our
money back.

Since each situation is unique we will offer general suggestions and guidelines that you can tailor
to your particular situation.

Effective consumerism starts when you are considering buying something, You are always ahead
if you select a recognized brand from a reputable

dealer. Before you take the item home be certain you understand both the warranty provisions, including the fine print, and the operating instructions. Hang on to sales slips and other proofs of purchase, such as charge card forms. If you pay by check, you not only have proof of purchase, but you also have the opportunity to stop payment if you find out immediately that the product is not satisfactory and the dealer is not inclined to help you.

Your first step in negotiating a consumer complaint is to make sure you are in the right. Did you play by the warranty rules and did you follow the operating instructions exactly?

If the answer is yes, you should organize all of the information you have that has anything to do with the problem. Include notes of what happened and the people you talked to at what time and date, as well as receipts, contracts, and the like. Keep this material current as the process goes along.

Take action as promptly as possible, while the facts are clear and before warranties expire. Visit the store or office in person, if possible, and personally state your problem. Stay calm and assertive and keep your anger or frustration in check. You need to take the offensive quickly since the seller is being asked to take something back for an exchange or give something in the form of a refund.

Very often this is all you have to do because reputable dealers automatically take back goods or make good on their agreements. But if you are not satisfied with the results after a reasonable time has elapsed, it is time to gear up for your second contact with someone of higher rank than the first person you complained to. This might be the store owner or a district manager or even the president of the company. (Most libraries have a volume called, *Standard & Poor's Register of Corporations*, in which you can find complete company addresses and the names of executive officers.)

Arm yourself with knowledge of your rights and of basic consumer law. Citing authorities such as the Fair Credit Billing Law or the Truth in Lending Law favorably increase your negotiating leverage.

Whenever you can, use the seller's own written statements from commercials or product literature. For example, if the seller's advertising boasts about the durability of the product and the one you bought fell apart, use the manufacturer's very words to put the seller on the defensive.

Just as with other negotiating, it is wise to set a deadline to prevent your opponent from having time to delay the process. Be clear in your demand that your opponent must give you satisfactory results within a designated time.

NEGOTIATING CONSUMER COMPLAINTS BY LETTER

If complaining in person or over the telephone is not possible or has not brought you the results you want, consider writing letters. Depending upon the nature of your complaint, the solution for which you are negotiating and where you are in the process, the letter could take a variety of forms. Most effective complaint letters, however, contain the following information.

1. Clearly state your case. Emphasize early what you want to be done; don't just complain about what went wrong.
2. Include all pertinent information in a history of the transaction with dates, names, and places.
3. Send copies of sales slips or receipts. *Don't* send originals.
4. Ask for a prompt response by a specific deadline.
5. Cite any law, ruling, or regulation that backs up your cause.
6. Explain your intended action if a satisfactory solution is not reached by the deadline. (We have advised against bluffing before and the advice applies here. Don't threaten to sue unless you are prepared to do so.)
7. Include your full name, address, and telephone number along with any other relevant identifying information, such as an account number.

Of course, your letter should be as businesslike as possible. Use firm, formal language and a compact, easy-to-read format. Particularly if your first letter has gone unanswered, consider sending this one by certified mail with return receipt requested. Proof that your letter was received could be important evidence if the matter does go to court or arbitration.

Consider sending copies of your letter to appropriate governmental agencies and professional associations such as the Better Business Bureau. Media outlets such as newspapers and local radio stations that have consumer advocate features may also get copies. Be sure to show on the face of the letter all the places to which you are sending copies. This information will increase your negotiating leverage since most businesses do not like to have their lack of performance to their customers publicized.

TWO OTHER SUGGESTIONS

First, if you find yourself in a position where your problem is not faulty merchandise but slow service, don't forget that your inconvenience and dissatisfaction can be used as leverage. As an example, Barbara ordered custom draperies and was told that the reason they were not delivered on the promised date was because the material had contained a flaw. Several weeks later, when the same excuse was given a second time, Barbara negotiated a lowered overall price as well as a firm installation date beyond which the draperies would not be accepted.

Second, don't allow yourself to be intimidated or bypassed. One woman who called to complain about a product was told to put her husband on the telephone. Fortunately, she did not fall for that one and said, "No, I'm the one who bought the product. You need to deal with me."

CHAPTER 12

Negotiating the Purchase of an Automobile

Almost every woman will have the occasion to purchase a new or used automobile. With inflation, this outlay has grown larger and can range from a few hundred dollars to many thousands of dollars. In addition, since the life expectancy of most cars is not too long, purchasing a car can become a frequent occurrence. It is therefore important to possess negotiating knowledge that will enable you to get that good deal most car dealers are constantly claiming they give.

SOME REPRESENTATIVE EXPERIENCES

One woman executive related her first experience as a car buyer. "It was a big step for me to go by myself to buy a car, and I needed to prove to myself that I could do it. I paid the full sticker price because I didn't know any better. Two years later

I traded cars again, but much more wisely that time."

Another professional woman described her first car buying experience and how she tried to use her lack of knowledge as an advantage.

"I told the salesman it was the first car I'd ever bought because my husband had always bought the cars and now I was divorced and on my own. I frankly told him I was nervous and unsure and would appreciate some tips. I knew this approach was risky because I could have set myself up as a pigeon, but at the same time I put the burden on him to be fair. I told him I was really trusting him but if I found out I could have made a better deal somewhere else I'd really be upset and I'd come back and hound him."

CHECK WITH MORE THAN ONE DEALER TO INCREASE NEGOTIATING LEVERAGE

Seldom, if ever, is it wise to buy a car from the first dealer you talk with. On the contrary, the wisest approach is to ask the first dealer to quote you a price for the car you are interested in. This price includes the gross sales price and the net price after reduction for any trade-in on your present car. Often dealers are reluctant to quote a price if they know you will be shopping around. They prefer to say that you should check with them last and they will meet or beat any other dealer's price.

At first blush this may appear to be fair. But what it does is insulate the dealer from quoting a price that may eventually be too low.

For example, assume you accept the dealer's

offer of meeting or beating any other dealer's price and there is only one other dealer in the city who sells the make of car you want. You go to the other dealer and he or she agrees to sell you the car you have in mind for $7,000. You go back to the first dealer and he drops the price to $6,900, a reduction of $100. The first dealer has lived up to the promise of meeting or beating any other dealer in town. You can then go back to the second dealer and try to get a further reduction below $6,900 and the second dealer may go for it. But you cannot then expect to go back to the first dealer and ask for a further reduction based upon the offer to meet or beat any other dealer's price because the first dealer has already done that with the offer of a $100 reduction.

GET DEALERS TO COMPETE FOR YOUR BUSINESS

In the foregoing example, if you got the first dealer to quote you a price for the car and then took that price to the second dealer, the second dealer would probably quote you a lower price than the first dealer. Taking the second dealer's price back to the first dealer should, in most instances, give you a further reduction.

If you want to increase the competition still further, shop for cars made by different car manufacturers. Each dealer will usually try even harder to see to it that you buy his make of car. John knows of a situation in which three dealers were competing for a sale and the price went straight down to below the dealer's cost, the dealers were so intent on making the sale.

Go to more than one dealer and be certain to let each dealer know that you will be visiting the others in order to see who offers the best price. This almost automatically increases your negotiating leverage, partly from the fear of losing your business and partly to satisfy their competitive appetite for taking business away from their competition. Remember, too, that dealers who service cars, and most do, want you as a regular customer for any maintenance and repair work and for possible car purchases in the future.

CREATE OPPORTUNITIES TO INCREASE YOUR LEVERAGE

Most car salespeople work on a commission basis, either completely or partially. They are therefore prone to wanting to sell even though they may be forced to shave the sale price down to such an extent that there is little profit for the dealer. You can therefore increase your negotiating leverage by taking advantage of the *salesperson's* fear of losing the commission. You can do this by stating valid reservations for not being able to purchase the car, such as, "I can't afford it," or "My husband won't let me spend that much," or "I don't like the color."

Take your husband or a friend with you so that you can carry on a conversation *within* earshot of the salesperson. This technique of speaking to the salesperson through another party is often a highly effective negotiating tactic that can bring surprising results. And if the salesperson responds to your negative comments, even though you are speaking to your husband or a friend, you know the technique is working.

If, for example, you say to your friend, "The price is too high for my budget," and the salesperson picks it up and says, "Oh don't worry about that. I'm sure we can work out a deal within your budget," you know that the salesperson is alert and your strategy is working. You have increased your leverage and thus your negotiating power.

Use this technique to get concessions from the dealer and follow up to make certain that these concessions are honored. You might remind the salesperson, "Okay, you said we could work out a deal within my budget. The most I can pay for the car is $6,000." You have now taken the offensive and the burden is clearly on the salesperson to produce.

AVOID INSTANT DECISIONS

Automobiles roll off the factory assembly line at an incredibly fast pace. Most car models can therefore be easily duplicated. Even comparable used cars can be found with a little searching and often at lower prices. As a consequence, unless there are other extenuating circumstances that make it necessary to buy immediately, it isn't wise to make an instant decision when buying a car. Resist any pressure from the dealer. Most dealers you have visited will call you in a day or two to follow up on the first conversation. If you were not satisfied with what they proposed when you visited, those calls present an opportunity to make your position known and seek further concessions.

USE DEALER'S COMMERCIALS TO YOUR ADVANTAGE

Take advantage of dealer's advertisements. If, for example, a dealer advertises that, "Nobody undersells us," or "We will beat any deal," be sure to take the dealer up on it. If you have a deal that is lower, point it out to the dealer who has advertised and also at the same time remind the dealer about the advertisement. This gives you negotiating momentum and places the dealer on the defensive. The dealer must either give you a lower price or distinguish your case from the advertisement, which you should not allow. If the dealer attempts it, keep going back to the advertisement. In most cases, if the dealer is reputable, the advertised claim will be honored. If not, you should seriously question whether you want to do business with that dealer.

IT IS THE NET CASH OUTLAY THAT COUNTS

It makes no difference whether the dealer decreases the gross price of the car or increases the trade-in allowance on any car you want to trade in. The important objective is the lowest possible net cash outlay. If the dealer will not increase the value of your trade-in by $500 but will reduce the gross price of the new car by $500, the result is the same. You will pay $500 less for the new car.

CHAPTER 13

Negotiating the Purchase of a House

Purchasing a house has become a very important investment decision due primarily to the tremendous appreciation in housing prices. In addition, many women, whether married or single, will have the occasion to buy at least one house.

There are essentially two important aspects when negotiating the purchase of a house. One is the cost of the house, which at today's prices is apt to be a significant amount. The other is financing the purchase. Unless the house is going to be paid for in cash, which is seldom the case, acquiring a loan at a favorable true loan cost is most certainly an important aspect. Negotiating loans has been fully covered in Chapter 10.

BE FULLY AWARE OF THE ROLE OF THE REAL ESTATE BROKER

At the outset, it is important to understand that the real estate broker has contracted in writing to represent the seller of the house, not you, the buyer. Although this may seem obvious, it is frequently overlooked to the detriment of the buyer because many experienced brokers are very good at winning the confidence of the buyer and making it seem as if they are actually working for the buyer. This situation frequently results in buyers letting their negotiating guards down. Once that happens, buyers usually wind up paying more for the house than is necessary. Hence, when negotiating the purchase of a house, always keep in mind that the broker is representing the seller and is going to try to get the highest possible price for the house.

Another reason why the broker is going after the highest possible price is that most brokers work on a commission that is based on the *gross* selling price of the house. The higher the selling price, therefore, the greater the broker's commission.

Brokers' commissions usually range between 6 to 10 percent of the gross sales price. Thus, a house that is offered for $100,000 will bring the broker a $10,000 commission if the rate is 10 percent, $6,000 if the rate is 6 percent. The broker knows that for every dollar the house is sold below the offering price, the broker will lose from 6 to 10 percent of that dollar.

Because the commission is based upon the gross sales price of the house, brokers are prone to initially setting a higher price than the fair market value of the house. This is a natural consequence since brokers obviously like to make as large a commission as possible. Sellers, too, ordinarily want to get the highest price possible for the house and are also prone to setting a higher offering price than the actual fair market value.

This practice, however, presents you with a unique negotiating opportunity. Since you can be reasonably assured that the price put on the house is higher than it will eventually sell for, you can comfortably, in most cases, make an offer for less than the asking price. What's more, your lower offer will be expected. Unless the house is really an unusually desirable property and is in great demand, the offering price normally leaves ample room for bargaining.

HASTE MAKES WASTE

The purchase of a house is definitely a long-term commitment, both from the standpoint of the term of the loan if the purchase is financed on borrowed money, and also the fact that real estate is normally not the type of investment that can be readily disposed of as, for example, common stock that can be sold simply by calling a stock broker. Houses are sometimes bought and sold soon after, but this is the exception rather than the rule; most quick sales are necessitated by such factors as a change of employment, death, or ill health. Such sales are often at a financial sacrifice for the seller. So don't rush into the purchase even if you have fallen in love with the house, and always approach the purchase as if you will be living in the house for a long time. This frame of mind will enable you to take greater care in negotiating the purchase and you will have greater assurance that you are proceeding with the purchase on terms and conditions that are favorable to you.

IMPORTANT INFORMATION TO GET EARLY

There are two important pieces of information you should acquire prior to any serious negotiating. One is how long the property has been listed for sale. You can usually obtain this information from the broker; it will help you to make assumptions that can materially assist you in the negotiation.

For example, once when John was asked to negotiate the purchase of a house, he learned from the broker that the house had been on the market for over a year. John therefore assumed there was a serious problem with the property, perhaps the offering price was too high or the house had defects that would be costly to repair. Upon inspecting the property, John determined that the primary reason the house had not sold had nothing to do with its physical condition. The problem was that the owner wanted to sell a large acreage with the house, which made the purchase price too high for most prospective buyers. Offers for the property were therefore hard to get and usually much lower than the asking price.

A second important piece of information is whether or not the seller has a pressing need to sell. If you learn that the seller has a pressing need to sell, perhaps due to such factors as retirement, a transfer out of the area, or a new house that is waiting to be moved into, you are alerted to the possibility that the seller may be experiencing anxiety over the need to sell the house. Under these conditions the seller is more apt to accept any reasonable offer even if it is substantially less than the asking price. On occasion a real estate firm may advertise "Must sell. Owner transferred," to give the impression that the seller is willing to sacrifice and accept less than the house's true value. Watch out for that technique. Make sure the reason for selling and the potential sacrifice are genuine.

BE FLEXIBLE

Flexibility almost automatically increases your negotiating leverage and thus your negotiating power. To illustrate, in the previous example of the house owner who wanted to sell the house with a large acreage, an offer was made to purchase the house at a much lower figure than the asking price, with only a few acres to go with the house. As part of the offer, an option was sought and obtained from the seller to purchase the remaining land over a period of several years. In other words, the house and a few acres were purchased outright and the purchaser also received the right to buy the remaining land later. Maintaining flexibility combined with the owner's need to sell thus allowed the buyer to acquire the property very reasonably.

CONTROL YOUR EMOTIONS

Controlling your emotions is a recurring theme throughout this book because it is so important. To illustrate, fear of loss is perhaps one of the greatest causes of negotiating failure and crops up at all levels of negotiating the purchase of a house. If a broker knows or senses that you are highly impressed with and attracted to the house, the broker may try to motivate you to purchase the house *at the asking price* by introducing fear of loss. "This house is a beauty and won't be on the market long," or "There are other people coming to see the house," are just a few examples of statements brokers may use to try to make buyers fear losing the house and thus motivate them to purchase the house at the offering price. These types of comments are generally a part of many brokers' standard operating procedure. Often, the potential buyer plays right into their hands by giving obviously favorable reactions when shown the house.

If you go through the house commenting on how great the kitchen is and how spacious the bedrooms are, for example, you are providing the broker with a perfect opportunity to interject comments such as those quoted above that are designed to motivate you to act fast or lose the opportunity to enjoy those features of the house that you are attracted to. So send your emotions on a vacation; don't take them to the property when you examine it. Remain calm and objective and, if you are looking at the property with other people, advise them not to display their feelings in front of the broker. You can confer privately with the other people, either out of the broker's presence or after you leave the property.

Frequently, a broker who is concerned about whether you have any real interest in the property will try harder to make the sale and will thus be more apt to be receptive to your offering price due to the broker's fear of losing the sale. If the broker attempts to play on your fear of loss routinely without any hint from you that you like the property, you can easily put the shoe on the other foot by saying, for example, "Oh, let the other people look at it. We have several other houses to look at." Now the broker is the one who may experience fear of losing the sale and the resulting commission, especially if you appear to be a good prospect. The broker might well be willing at this point to even suggest that you make an offer lower than the listed selling price.

Remember, when the broker goes to the seller, chances are good that the seller will rely heavily on the broker's opinion and advice as to whether your offering price should be accepted. Thus, if you have motivated the broker to agree to your offering price there is a much better chance that the broker will be able to convince the seller to accept it. In this way, you can virtually make the broker your ally in acquiring the property at your offering price.

LOOK FOR DEPRECIATING FACTORS

Always depreciate the seller's offering price by any adverse discoveries. Take along a pencil and paper and list each adverse factor as you go through the house. When it comes time to discuss price, carefully relate each one separately. This accumulation technique will have a greater depreciation impact, which is the reason why thorough inspection of the house should be undertaken.

If you are married, it is a good idea for both you and your husband to examine the property together. Four eyes that are working toward the same objective are better than two. Between you, you are more apt to catch any defects. One of you may notice the crack in the basement wall that the other missed.

GAINING SMALL CONCESSIONS CAN MEAN LARGE SAVINGS

Too often, the significance of gaining small concessions is overlooked, particularly when the price of the house is high. Why go to the trouble of getting a $500 reduction in the purchase price when you are willing to invest $100,000 to buy the property? But translated into actual dollar savings, small price reductions can add up.

For instance, the cost to repay $500 at 9½ percent over a thirty-year period is $1,515.60. That is how much you would save on a simple $500 reduction in the purchase price if you obtained a thirty-year loan at 9½ percent. On a $1,000 price reduction at 9½ percent over thirty years, you would save $3,027.60.[1]

---

1. Interest on a house loan is deductible for federal income tax purposes. The savings given here are before computation of any tax increase due to a decreased interest deduction.

MAKING THE PURCHASE OFFER

In Chapter 7 we discussed making the offer and counteroffer. It is appropriate to talk about this subject again in specific relationship to house buying.

Offers to purchase houses are normally in writing and frequently on printed forms readily available in most areas. In fact, most brokers usually carry a supply and can whip one out on the spot, fill in the blanks, and ask you to sign. This is not a tentative offer but a real commitment. Once your signature is affixed, you are legally bound to stand by your offer unless the offer is rejected by the seller.

The terms of the written offer govern the terms of the sale. Thus, whatever specific terms you have negotiated should be carefully spelled out in the written offer. Once the seller accepts your written offer neither you nor the seller can vary the terms unless you both mutually agree on the variance.

For example, not long ago John negotiated the purchase of a large parcel of real estate. The terms and conditions were clearly set forth in the written offer. The property was purchased on a land contract, which means that instead of obtaining a loan to finance the purchase from a lender, the purchaser and seller entered into a contract wherein the purchaser agreed to pay the seller the purchase price, less any cash down payment, over a designated period of years at a stated interest rate.

The attorney for the seller, when he drafted the land contract, included provisions in the contract that were not contained in the written offer, and also attempted to alter other aspects of the written offer. When it was called to the attorney's attention that the terms of the written offer couldn't be changed, he reluctantly agreed to follow precisely the terms contained in the offer.

Be certain that whatever the finally negotiated terms are, they are included in the written offer. If they are not and the offer is accepted by the seller, you cannot later add any terms that were omitted from the written offer so that any favorable concessions you gained from your negotiating will be for nothing.

By way of further illustration, assume you decide that you do not want to pay any higher interest rate than 9 percent on any loan required to finance the purchase of the house. In addition, you gain the concession that the kitchen appliances, the refrigerator and stove will remain as part of the house and be included as part of the purchase price. (This tacking-on technique, incidentally, is an excellent way to gain reductions in the purchase price without actually reducing the cash price. Assume that you agree on a price of $75,000 for the house with the refrigerator and stove remaining as part of the house. Assume also that the cost of purchasing new appliances would be $500. You have effected a $500 savings by tacking on those appliances.)

Your written offer, then, should clearly state that your offer is conditioned on your being able to obtain a loan at 9 percent or less. The offer should also clearly state that both the refrigerator and stove will remain as part of the property with no increase in the $75,000 purchase price.

Always explain to the broker your reasons for making the offer for the price you have determined. Don't take for granted that the broker already knows the basis for your offer even though you may have already discussed the reasons. Reexplain the reasons for your offer at the time you make it. And even if the broker is fully aware, repeating them will act as reinforcement. Remember, you want the broker to be your ally in convincing the seller to accept your offer.

SET A TIME LIMIT ON YOUR OFFER AND KEEP IT SHORT

Recently an individual who sought John's advice about a large parcel of property he was attempting to buy, made an offer that allowed the seller to think over the offer and let the buyer know if it was acceptable as soon as possible. John advised the individual that this was, from a negotiating standpoint, clearly a mistake. The seller could spend the time seeking other buyers who were willing to pay a higher price for the property and, if none could be found, to eventually decide to accept the first offer. The person seeking John's advice had thus allowed the seller the luxury of keeping his options open, an ideal situation for any seller to be in and one that you, as the buyer, should avoid. Always set a time limit, usually a matter of two to five days, for acceptance of your offer. This puts pressure on the seller to either accept your offer or reject it without the opportunity to shop around for a higher bidder.

HOW TO TREAT COUNTEROFFERS

When you make a written offer for the house, the seller may come back with what is legally known as a counteroffer. This frequently happens in house transactions. The counteroffer is normally in writing, often right on the same document as the offer, and modifies the offer in one or more respects.

To illustrate, assume that you make an offer to purchase a house for $50,000 and, as part of your offer, the seller is required to pay for any cost of repairs to the roof. The price is acceptable to the seller but the seller wants to limit any cost of roof repairs to $500. The seller therefore submits a counteroffer that sets a $500 limit to any roof repairs. That counteroffer is really a rejection of your offer. You can either forget the whole matter, renew your original offer, make another counteroffer or accept the seller's counteroffer, in which, in this latter case, a binding contract exists between you and the seller to purchase the house.

If you adjust the seller's counteroffer by, for example, increasing the seller's liability for any roof repair to, say, $700, you have made a counteroffer to the seller's counteroffer to your offer. The seller again has the option of accepting or rejecting your counteroffer. This can go on and on and sometimes does, with either side making numerous offers and counteroffers.

The matter is simplified in Table 13.1. The boxes on the left represent you, the buyer. The boxes on the right represent the seller.

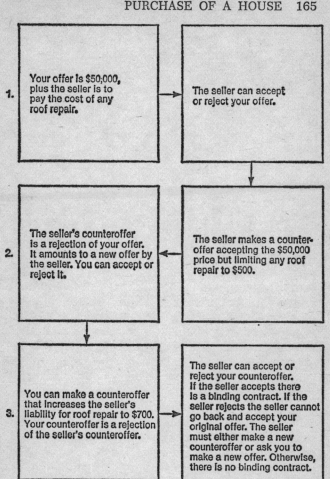

1. Your offer is $50,000, plus the seller is to pay the cost of any roof repair.

The seller can accept or reject your offer.

2. The seller's counteroffer is a rejection of your offer. It amounts to a new offer by the seller. You can accept or reject it.

The seller makes a counteroffer accepting the $50,000 price but limiting any roof repair to $500.

3. You can make a counteroffer that increases the seller's liability for roof repair to $700. Your counteroffer is a rejection of the seller's counteroffer.

The seller can accept or reject your counteroffer. If the seller accepts there is a binding contract. If the seller rejects the seller cannot go back and accept your original offer. The seller must either make a new counteroffer or ask you to make a new offer. Otherwise, there is no binding contract.

Table 13.1

CHAPTER 14

Negotiating the Purchase of Commercial or Investment Real Estate

Buying commercial or investment real estate is an area that many women are either already in or will be getting into as time progresses. We are using the term *commercial* to mean both property purchased for any business use, such as a retail store, and property used for industrial use, such as manufacturing products that are sold to retail businesses or to other businesses that assemble them with other products, for example, a company that manufactures radios to be installed in automobiles.

We are using the term *investment property* to mean any real estate (other than a house) that is not directly purchased for commercial or industrial use at the time of purchase but is held for later sale at, hopefully, a profit.

There are numerous similarities between negotiating a house purchase and negotiating the pur-

chase of commercial or investment real estate.
You do not, for example, want to rush into the
purchase, and should get as much early information about the property as possible prior to negotiating. In addition, you should be flexible, control
your emotions and look for depreciating discoveries that will assist you in bringing the price of the
property down. There are, however, interesting
and useful twists to negotiating the purchase of
commercial or investment real estate that you
should keep in mind when tackling the negotiating.

BROKERS' COMMISSIONS ARE USUALLY HIGHER

At the outset, commissions charged by brokers are
usually higher on commercial or investment property than that charged for the sale of a house.
From a negotiating standpoint, there is a greater
likelihood that the broker will try harder to make
the sale, and will be more likely to suffer fear of
losing the sale. Moreover, the broker's fear of loss
is frequently heightened by knowledge that other
brokers are out trying to sell the same property
whenever it is on a multiple listing basis. This
increases the chances that the broker will recom-
mend that the seller seriously consider accepting
any reasonable purchase offer.

Another factor that can increase the broker's
fear of losing the sale is that the price of commercial or investment property is often higher than
the price of the average house, simply because the
property is larger and may have buildings and
other improvements. So combining the higher

price with the higher broker's commissions means that the broker stands to make more money on the sale or lose the opportunity to make more money if the broker fails to make the sale. Never lose sight of this factor when you negotiate the purchase of commercial or investment property because it increases your negotiating leverage. Obviously, if the broker thinks you are a good prospective buyer and you have submitted what the broker feels is a reasonable offer, in most cases it is to the broker's advantage to work hard to get the seller to accept your offer.

THE SELLER'S LEAD-OUT PRICE CAN PROVIDE YOU WITH A NEGOTIATING EDGE

Prior to offering the property for sale, the seller and the seller's broker will arrive at a price at which to list the property. That is the price the broker will quote you when you come calling. What's more, that price sets the upper limit. You can be reasonably sure, in most instances, that the price is higher than the actual fair market value. Again, the seller obviously would like to make as much as possible on the sale and the broker will try to sell the property for the highest price possible to get the highest commission possible. Your offer can therefore be less than the price asked by the seller, which provides you with a definite edge in the bargaining. Not only can you frame your lower offer on terms and conditions that are most favorable to you but also you can expect that most of those terms will be accepted by the seller.

To illustrate, John was negotiating the purchase

of a large parcel of investment property for a client. It was a farm that was in a rapidly developing area. An offer was made for about 20 percent less than the seller's offering price. In addition, as part of the offer, John's client was willing to pay 20 percent of the purchase price in cash with the balance payable over a period of 30 years at a designated interest rate. This approach of stringing out the 80 percent balance of the purchase price over thirty years allowed John's client to pay a relatively small amount of principal and interest each year, let's say, for purposes of illustration, $10,000. To limit the seller from seeking other offers, a very short time limit for acceptance of the offer was specified. The short time limit also created fear of loss by the seller as the deadline drew nearer.

Prior to the expiration of John's client's offer, the seller made a counteroffer that accepted the purchase price, the amount of the down payment, and the interest rate. The only variation was the proposal that the remaining balance be paid within 10 years instead of 30 years.

Since John's client intended to sell the property in three to five years anyway, a counteroffer was made to the seller's counteroffer that spelled out that John's client was willing to pay off the remaining balance within 10 years as long as the annual payments remained the same as if the remaining balance were to be paid over the thirty-year period. In other words, John's client agreed to pay the remaining balance within ten years but only at $10,000 per year with any remaining balance at the end of ten years to be paid in full. The result was that John's client was able to purchase the property for the down payment and the annual payments John's client sought. Since John's client intended to sell the land within three to five years anyway, the 10 year payment requirement was an irrelevant factor from the buyer's standpoint.

The opportunity to do this type of bargaining was due in large part to the advantage enjoyed as a result of the seller's price setting. You can enjoy a similar advantage because the seller's lead-out price allows you to plan the type of strategy that is in your best interests or the best interests of your client.

MOST INITIAL OFFER TERMS AND CONDITIONS ARE ACCEPTED

Notice that in the previous experience that virtually all of John's client's terms were accepted by the seller except the number of years of payment of the entire balance. This is a common occurrence in negotiating the purchase of commercial or investment real estate where the seller sets the initial price. The basic reason is that the seller becomes oriented to selling the property once it is listed for sale and will therefore raise objections only to terms and conditions that the seller cannot live with. In addition, the number of buyers that are shopping for commercial or investment property is normally small. Hence, when a qualified buyer comes along the seller is more likely to accept any reasonable terms and conditions of a purchase offer.

As a further example, if a seller offers investment property for $4,000 per acre and the potential purchaser offers $3,500 per acre, the seller may not consider the $500-per-acre difference significant enough to reject the offer unless there exists a great demand for the property. This type of demand situation is not common for most commercial or investment real estate.

Don't be reluctant to specify and offer terms that you consider reasonable. In the usual situation, most will be accepted, and you will only have to negotiate the one or two terms that the seller did not accept.

DON'T DISCLOSE YOUR MOTIVE FOR BUYING THE PROPERTY

When negotiating the purchase of commercial or investment property, it is best not to disclose to the seller why you are purchasing the property, for two reasons. First, you may unnecessarily enlighten the seller on a possible use for the property that the seller hadn't thought of and thus cause the seller to either seek a higher price or even take the property off the market so that the seller can use it for the purposes you disclosed. Second, the seller may either directly or indirectly reveal your intended use to others who are already interested in the property or who may become interested upon learning why you want it. A bidding war may result, forcing the price of the property upward, perhaps even over the seller's original asking price. As a consequence, your negotiating task will become much more difficult.

On occasion you may have to disclose your intended use. John encountered such a situation in a negotiation in which a substantial portion of the property was used by the seller for the seller's business. Although the seller was willing to sell all of the property, he wanted to continue to use a portion for a designated time period. The seller, therefore, wanted to be sure that the intended use of the rest of the property would not conflict with his present use. Consequently, disclosure of the intended use of the property became a necessity.

If asked to explain the intended use, give a general reply such as that you're buying the property for investment purposes. In most instances, it is your business why you are buying the property.

It is not wise, however, to decline to give a reason for buying the property because this may make the seller suspicious that you have some unique use that the seller should know about. This may make the seller hesitant to sell or cause the seller to increase the price, either of which would make your negotiating task far more difficult.

LITTLE THINGS CAN MEAN A LOT

C. Northcote Parkinson wrote that "the world is full of people who . . . knowing nothing of millions [of dollars] are well accustomed to think in thousands [of dollars]."[1] Experience has shown this to be correct when it comes to negotiation. We all tend to concentrate on smaller sums of money to the exclusion of large sums. Recognizing this reality can lead you to excellent negotiating results, especially where it concerns the purchase

---

1. C. Northcote Parkinson, *Parkinson's Law* (New York: Ballantine Books, 1964), p. 39.

of commercial or investment real estate with large price tags.

For example, John negotiated the acquisition of a sizable piece of land for a client who wanted it for investment purposes. An offer was made to purchase the property for a price that was considerably lower than the price asked by the seller. The seller was concerned about payment of title insurance premiums that amounted to several hundred dollars, and he was also worried about getting the money from that year's grain crop that was then growing on the property. The seller proposed that the cost of title insurance be divided equally between the buyer and seller and that the seller be allowed to keep the money from that year's grain crop. Both proposals were immediately accepted.

Making allowance for both the title insurance and grain crop, although relatively insignificant in comparison to the total purchase price, meant a lot to the seller. Indeed, if these two aspects had not been settled to the seller's satisfaction, the entire transaction might have been in jeopardy.

Always bear in mind that whether you are buying or selling commercial or investment property, chances are your opponent will place important emphasis on the smaller, peripheral financial aspects of the transaction. But you should concentrate on the large amounts, namely, the purchase price, the method of payment and the interest rate in the event you will borrow money to make the purchase or purchase the property on contract. It is usually, for instance, wiser and less expensive to agree to pay a title insurance premium of several hundred dollars if you can get a one percent drop in the interest rate on a long-term contract to purchase the property. The savings in interest over the contract term, in most cases, will far exceed the cost of the title insurance. You should, of course, not depend upon chance and actually calculate what the interest rate reduction will amount to over the terms of the contract. This calculation should be done prior to the time you negotiate so that you will know precisely the cost of any concessions you make during the negotiation, such as the payment of title insurance relative to the savings you will obtain from any interest reduction.